We Need Not Walk Alone

After the Death of a Child

Edited By
Mary Cleckley
Elizabeth Estes
Priscilla Norton

Second Edition

Cover photography by
Joseph Robert Pfeiffer

The Compassionate Friends
Oak Brook, IL
1992

Published in the United States by The Compassionate Friends, Oak Brook, Illinois.

Library of Congress Catalog Number 90-80297

ISBN 1-878615-00-9

Second Edition — 1992

CONTENTS

CHAPTER I
THE COMPASSIONATE FRIENDS

CREDO

We need not walk alone. We are The Compassionate Friends. We reach out to each other with love, with understanding and with hope. Our children have died at all ages and from many different causes, but our love for our children unites us. Your pain becomes my pain just as your hope becomes my hope. We come together from all walks of life, from many different circumstances. We are a unique family because we represent many races and creeds. We are young and we are old. Some of us are far along in our grief, but others still feel a grief so fresh and so intensely painful that we feel helpless and see no hope. Some of us have found our faith to be a source of strength; some of us are struggling to find answers. Some of us are angry, filled with guilt or in deep depression; others radiate an inner peace. But whatever pain we bring to this gathering of The Compassionate Friends, it is pain we will share just as we share with each other our love for our children. We are all seeking and struggling to build a future for ourselves, but we are committed to building that future together as we reach out to each other in love and share the pain as well as the joy, share the anger as well as the peace, share the faith as well as the doubts and help each other to grieve as well as to grow. We need not walk alone. We are The Compassionate Friends.

REFLECTIONS OF SIMON
BUTTERFLIES

"Have you seen the butterflies at the rainbow's end?" so goes a verse in a 16th Century English sonnet. As we gather here in Tulsa this July afternoon, drawn from every corner of the North American continent to honour our children on this very first National Children's Memorial Day, I can say to you as the Founder of THE COMPASSIONATE FRIENDS, yes, I have seen the butterflies!

Fifteen years ago, prompted by a Time-Life magazine article about the ministry of The Compassionate Friends in the United Kingdom, Arnold and Paula Shamres of Hialeah, Florida, stretched out a hand across the North Atlantic that they might make our vision, theirs. Forsaking London's November snow, I flew out to join them. Their grief was total. Their hearts were seemingly irreparably broken by the death of their daughter Gabrielle, and they were struggling in the Valley of the Shadow. But news from England gave them hope. Perhaps the dawn of their recovery was about to break, and I met a couple of great compassion and vision.

To Arnold and Paula Shamres for their courage, foresight, and compassion we owe a tremendous debt of gratitude. But this afternoon we also honour all those men and women from every state in the Union who through the redeeming power of their children's love have had the courage and willpower to ensure the growth of this great family of THE COMPASSIONATE FRIENDS. We have indeed encircled the world with compassion!

The miracle of love which you are all a part has been and remains a costly one. Let us not deny that! But the needs remain as great as ever and bereaved parents the world over require the healing love and hope which only you, THE COMPASSIONATE FRIENDS, can offer.

On this our National Children's Memorial Day let it not be forgotten that it is not only love which binds us as one. Today, we all share in a special sense of pride in and love for our children; and they alone will enable us to count the butterflies at the rainbow's end.

May God richly bless you and may your child's love enable you to find fulfillment and peace.

Simon Stephens
Founder, The Compassionate Friends
From the first National Children's
Memorial Day in Tulsa, Oklahoma, 1987

LETTER FROM JOE

Let me introduce my wife Iris and myself, Joe. We are two of the original Compassionate Friends and, for my sins, I was the Founder Chairman. I would like to do a regular article for the newsletter bringing to all our CFs the early days of the "the Society," which is what we used to affectionately call it. Herewith the first installment.

The family was engaged in the usual morning hassle as we washed, dressed, ate and finally shared a moment as the children left for school. We were four - Iris and Joe, parents, Angela (the elder of our children, aged nearly fifteen), and Kenneth (the younger, nearly twelve). The youngsters departed and then minutes later, as we prepared to leave too, the telephone rang. I picked it up. A voice said, "There's been an accident. Kenneth has been taken to hospital by ambulance." We rushed to the hospital, convincing each other that it was nothing worse than a broken limb, but within a short time we knew that it could be serious. He was unconscious; later we were told that he had suffered major head injuries with resultant brain damage. We were face-to-face with death. Elsewhere in the hospital was another boy, Bill Henderson, suffering from cancer. His parents had nursed him through a long illness, at his bedside day and night. We discovered later that the Henderson family, Bill and Joan, the parents, Andrew and Bill, their sons, and daughters Shone and Susan, and ourselves were all known to the Reverend David Dale, a minister in the United Reformed Church.

Standing back from the constant group of relatives and friends around Kenneth's bed in the Intensive Care Unit was another young man in clerical garb, the Rev. Simon Stephens. He simply said, "If I can help, I am here all of the time." Eventually we asked, "Will you pray for Kenneth?" and when he did so, he mentioned Bill Henderson. Thus we came to know that somewhere in this vast hospital another boy lay dying, another family hoped and prayed. It was not to be. Kenneth died on 23 May 1968 - a day now indelibly stamped in our memory. Bill Henderson died a few days later.

Iris suggested that we send flowers to Joan and Bill; we did not then know the significance of that act but, looking back, it might be said that The Compassionate Friends started there. Joan and Bill telephoned their thanks and we met for a cup of tea. Together, midst freely-flowing tears, the four of us were able for the first time to speak openly of our children without feelings of guilt that we were endlessly repeating the virtues of our children and of our vanished hopes for the future. Together, we were all able to accept for the first time the words used by many well-meaning friends - but rejected almost universally by parents who have lost a beloved child - "I understand." We did understand, all four of us, and in the immensity of our grief (and in reality is there any other tragedy of quite this enormity?) we all suffered together.

We were helping each other - a telephone call in the blackest hour brought love and help immediately to the door; the regular family visits where the younger members reminded us constantly of their needs and dragged us back to the role of parent, and where the occasionally humorous incidents induced the first smiles, and even laughs - all these played their part in our journey through the experience of overwhelming grief. We were learning to live a little again. It did not happen overnight, nor even with years, but it had started.

Simons Stephens, who had kept close contact with us, spotted it first. He said, "You are helping each other in a way I, and virtually everyone else, am unable to do, because of your shared experience; do you think it would work with other bereaved parents?" We put it to the test. We wrote to, and subsequently visited, a West Indian family who had lost a young child in a road accident. It worked. We became friends.

Simon then suggested a meeting of a number of recently-bereaved parents, and the initial coming-together took place in January 1969 in a room at the Coventry and Warwickshire Hospital, a place with poignant memories for most of us; returning to the hospital itself was, you might say, a hurdle which we needed to surmount.

In the event, six people were present - Bill and Joan Henderson, Betty Rattigan, Simon Stephens, Iris and myself. We talked about an organization which would try to help other bereaved parents. But the number of child-deaths in the UK was dauntingly large - would we be able to cope with what might become an overwhelming demand on our time? We decided to try.

What about a name? The word "compassion" had featured frequently in our conversations, and eventually "The Society of Compassionate Friends" emerged. It sounded right then, and now, fifteen years later and in a slightly shorter form, it still sounds right - perhaps even inspired.

To round off this opening part of the history of The Compassionate Friends, I would like to record the names of that first committee. They were Honorary President, Simon Stephens; Chairman, Joe Lawley; Secretary, Betty Rattigan; Coordinator, Joan Henderson; Treasurer, Bill Henderson; Member and Visitor, Iris Lawley.

With love, Joe Lawley

Joe Lawley
TCF, England

FAR BEYOND THE CLOUDS

Far beyond the clouds above
A special garden grows with love.
Special flowers of many blends
Are the children of The Compassionate Friends.

Sam Rosenberg
TCF, Louisville, KY

VALLEY OF THE BUTTERFLIES

There is a green, sun-drenched valley -
Light with the scent of clover and lilacs -
Where the butterflies dance.
Leaping and swooping, they reflect colors
Of every hue and dimension.
There are monarchs and skippers,
Swallowtails and delicate spring azures.
Each dances its unique pattern
Of flits, circles and dives.
Stretching its fragile wings toward the clouds
Or brushing its feet on the succulent grass.

There are no roads, paths, or gates
To broach the valley's entrance;
Yet it is visited often in thoughts and dreams.
Every parent who has sent forth a child
And vainly waited for its return
Comes seeking in the valley of the butterflies
And there finds a beautiful spirit,
Stretching its wings to the clouds
And brushing its feet on the grass,
Dancing in swoops, flits and dives,
Drying its dewy wings in the warm sunshine of
forever.

Marcia Alig
TCF - Princeton Jct., NJ

WHY BUTTERFLIES

Since the early centuries of the Christian Church, the butterfly has symbolized the resurrection and life after death. The caterpillar signifies life here on earth; the cocoon, death; and the butterfly, the emergence of the dead into a new, beautiful and freer existence. Frequently, the butterfly is seen with the word "Nika," which means victory. Elisabeth Kubler-Ross movingly tells of seeing butterflies drawn all over the walls of the children's dormitories in the World War II concentration camps. Since Elisabeth believes in the innate intuitiveness of children, she concludes that these children knew their fate and were leaving us a message. The Compassionate Friends has adopted the butterfly as one of its symbols - a sign of hope to us that our children are living in another dimension with greater beauty and freedom - a comforting thought to many.

From the TCF Newsletter
Author unknown

A VOICE IS CALLING

How can we learn to laugh again when we've lost a part of ourselves?

Our name is legion—those of us who must learn to live with less than we had—for whatever reason.

"I should be thankful for what is left—but I'm not. I don't want to live with less." These are our words when something vital is subtracted from our lives.

It's so hard to be thankful. We've lost a child and we are left empty.

How do we rejoice in hope, or learn to be patient in our tribulation? Some days it's so dark, we can't see the way.

In our youth, we like to believe we are a marble column that lives—that we can never be chipped or broken. We want our building stones to fit without mortar.

We'll be young forever with our loved ones near and safe—clinging to health, beauty, to athletic prowess, to what we prize.

We belong to the trumpet corps, leading the parade. When we have played the trumpet, we don't want to play the piccolo.

"You will be changed"—these are some of the cruelest of all words. No more trumpets—not ever.

The way back from the edge is different for each of us. To give up a part of ourselves is a small death. How do we learn to walk on crutches when yesterday we won the race?

"My soul is weary of my life," Job said. "I'm afraid of all my sorrows."

The way back from the deepest pit is to know that our minds and souls are what we are—not a transient physical perfection or the swiftest runner.

Grief is a slow wisdom. With it comes acceptance of the truth—what we have lost is gone forever—but there is a place called Memory to go back to and rest for a while when the truth hurts too much.

I may be less, but I'm me. I'm like a snowflake proud for the time I am given.

Sing no sad songs for me. Laughter is the healer's hand on my shoulder. To laugh is to celebrate the miracle of being alive.

I'm broken, but I'm on fire. I am needed.

Laughter is as necessary to life as the plow to a field. Every laughing face is beautiful and lights up my darkest corners.

I'm me—the best of me is left, and I'll find an orchestra that needs a piccolo.

If you would bring me a gift, make it a smile—and I'll have one waiting for you.

I'm thankful because I hear a voice calling my name—"Come on in! The water's fine!"

Written for The Compassionate Friends
by Kathryn Patton
Atlanta, Ga.

CHILD

Who is "the child" of Compassionate Friends?
Who knows that secret being of many beings, that life of many lives?
Entity of love, uniting hearts in pain,
Bringing hope to the hopeless, relief to the mourning-weary.
Your passing, unwanted transition, from here to untouchable eternity,
Plunging lives into despair - the irony - you, child of love,
Whose death heaped dark agonies upon those who carried you
In wombs of brilliant expectation, preparing for birth, for life. Came death.
So, yet unfulfilled, our minds seek respite.
Who are you, child of Compassionate Friends?

The voice is your child's, my child's.
It falls recognized on the ears of its mothers, its fathers
And softly, lovingly, knowing our pain and doubt
As once it knew our touch, our joy, our tears, it now knows
Our need for meaning in the meaningless, joy in the pain,
And it replies, reassuring, "I am your child . . . and your child."

I was but weeks from conception, but days from birth. My birthdays were few. My birthdays were many.
I am your baby. Your child. Your son. Your daughter: child, adult.
But no age of fruition, each age not enough.
All ages with hopes unrealized, goals unachieved, love unexpressed.
Potential unreached, paths undetermined. I died too soon.

My death: accident . . . illness . . . sudden . . . predicted . . .
At home . . . nearby . . . distant.
You were with me . . . I was alone but knew your loving presence.
I have watched you live it, relive it, again . . . again.
I have seen the fear, the guilt, the longing, the depression,
The anger, the hope, the valleys, and later, the hilltops. No mountains here.

And the questions, always unanswered, always repeated.
Could I have removed the anquish, the unrelenting ache
That bespoke my loss, I would and more:
I would restore . . . oh, I would drench you in my love again,
Surround you with my laughter, enrich you with the fulfillments and pleasures
My long life would have brought you -
Whose own lives would have been freely given to spare mine.

Yet, given no choice there, you found another . . .
You committed your lives to others like you:
Those mothers and fathers with whose offspring I dwell
Whose children are my family as their parents are now yours.
United, we wait for you . . . not anxious, but joyful, for we live in beauty,
Feeling here, the warmth of your love shared, your hope shared.
We are "the child," the unification of your loss:
A child of love manifested in your compassion, a child alive in your choice
To go on . . . together.

Joe Rousseau
National TCF President

CHAPTER II
WHAT IT'S ALL ABOUT

STRANGERS

Strangers walk the road with me
Strangers who are unaware
Strangers look at me and see
Only heaviness to share

And I turn my hurt aside
Waiting for one healing touch
But the strangers frown and chide
That I count my grief too much

Only now and then a friend
Someone who is grieving too -
Helps my broken life to mend.
And perhaps that friend is you?

Sascha Wagner
TCF, Des Moines, IA

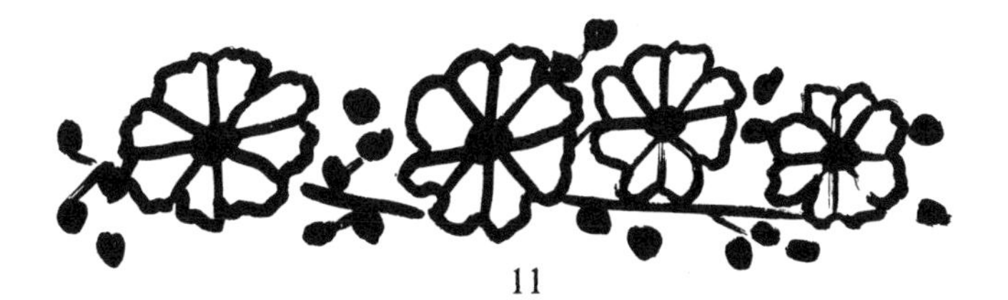

COMPASSION

I cry when a tear rolls down your cheek
I agonize when you weep
I know that you question, I know that you pray
That you scream at night in your sleep.

I'm aware of your quavering voice when you speak
Of your blank, straightforward stare
I know of your pain, your depression, your guilt
That you search for "a face" everywhere.

I watch as you walk with your head bowed low
With despair written over your face
I hear the quick sigh, the internal cry
I know how you wearily pace.

I see how you search for a sign, for some hope
That the light will still shine in your life
I know how you live, I know that you die
From the harsh words that wound like a knife.

I empathize most with your loneliness now
Even though you're not always alone
I see the rapture as you speak your child's name
For I've lost a son of my own.

Charmaine Stickel
TCF, Pittsburgh, PA

WE'RE ALIKE, YOU AND I

We're alike, you and I.
We've never met. Our faces would be those of strangers if we met. We would barely perceive the other's presence if we passed on our walk through the mists. We're unknown to each other until the terrible words have been spoken: "MY CHILD DIED."

We're alike, you and I. We measure time in seconds and eternities. We try to go forward to yesterday. Tomorrows are for whole people, and we are incomplete now. The tears after a time turn inward to become invisible to all save you and me. Our souls are rumpled from wrestling with demons and doubts and unanswerable prayers: "GIVE ME BACK MY CHILD."

We're alike, you and I.
The tears that run down your face are my tears and the wound in your soul is my pain, too. We need time, but time is our enemy for it carries us farther and farther from our lost child. And we cry out: "HELP ME."

We're alike, you and I.
And we need each other. Don't turn away, but give me your hand and for a time we can cease to be strangers and become what we truly are, a family closer than blood, united by a bond that was forced upon us—but a bond that can make us stronger, still wounded to be sure, but stronger for our sorrows are shared.

"WE NEED NOT WALK ALONE."

Judy Dickey
TCF, Greenwood, IN

STORYTELLERS IN THE CIRCLE OF WEAVERS

They come to tell their story
in the circle of weavers.
Because it is a story of love,
it is also a story of pain.
They tell how they wove their fabric,
with care, with many threads.
They tell how the fabric
was ripped beyond repair.
The sound of that long, final tear
is in their voices, and in the air.
It follows them relentlessly, everywhere.

The silence at the end of the story
could be the end.
But in the circle of weavers,
it is not the end.
Torn threads begin to stir.
Back and forth,
across and around the circle,
the weaving begins.
The threads are torn, and broken,
But there is life and power
in the weaving of them.

Pain and loss can be respected.
They cannot be changed.
But new cloth can be woven,
of caring, and understanding,
Even with broken threads,
In the circle of weavers.

Elizabeth Morris
TCF, Concord, MA

THANKS

Thanks to the friend who did know the "right words" to say: "There is a group in town that might help you."

Thanks to the parent who somehow found the courage to call that phone number and find out about "that group."

Thanks to the mother who went to that first meeting knowing it would really hurt to talk - and talked.

Thanks to the dad who said after the first meeting that he could never come back - but did.

Thanks to the parent who, at the fifth meeting, put her arms around a "new one" and said: "They really can help."

Thanks to the mom who, for the first time, was again able to bake cookies - for her "Compassionate Friends."

Thanks to the homemaker who could never talk in front of people - who became a facilitator.

Thanks to the six-foot father who cried in front of the other men—and didn't say he was sorry.

Because of you, we will be able to help someone we don't even know - next month.

John DeBoer
TCF, Greater Omaha, NE

HOW TCF WORKS

The Compassionate Friends is a self-help group for parents who have experienced the death of a child. The primary method is by providing sharing groups, but newsletters, lending libraries, guest speakers, and telephone friends are part of most chapter programs. Present at every meeting are parents who have survived and can model that it is possible to do so. There is no elaborate structure, no affiliation with any religion, and any contributions are entirely voluntary.

Members are at all stages of recovery and fluctuating among them. Some have deep religious faith, some have lost theirs, many are adrift. Even a small chapter is apt to include some who are currently receiving professional help or who have had such help in the past, in addition to participating in TCF. In the group, one of the first great learnings is this: I have not been singled out for this unspeakable affliction. There are all these others, and, as one gets to know them, they are fine people with beautiful children also. The absolute isolation that bereaved parents feel starts to break down into identification with the group. At some point "Why me?" and "Why my child?" can begin to give way to "Why us?" and "Why all our children?"

Attendance at TCF meetings brings us together with many other parents who feel the same way and with parents who have succeeded in resolving many of the problems. Some meetings include a short portion giving cognitive knowledge about some aspect of grief and healing (speaker, film, book review) and most chapters also have a lending library of books and tapes, but it is the sharing that brings parents back time after time. This is often the first group that they have felt comfortable with and may even be the first social contact.

It is, of course, the "me too's" that are magic. Someone in the group will have felt "that way" too. And another part of the magic is that someone else won't have felt that way at all. We learn that there is no right way and no wrong way. Each has to find a way that works. We give no ANSWER. We give lots of answers. Pick one.

The most important things that TCF offers are the endless capacity to listen with true empathy and the reassurance that one is not "going crazy." People come together with nothing else in common but their bereavement, and nothing else matters. We listen to each other's stories told over and over as each tries to convey the specialness of the lost child, to deal with the events surrounding the death itself, the bitterness and alienation that remain, the disappointment over anticipated support that does not materialize. We do not live up to the expectations of society; we are uncomfortable for friends and fellow-workers; we think that perhaps they are right and that we should be "putting it all behind us" and "getting on with our lives." We pretend, but we are frightened.

Some doctors prescribe for our "nerves" and some clergy tell us "It's God will." Even our parents, our brothers and sisters, think we should be over it, and our other children appear to be going on with their lives as though nothing has happened, or else they are in deep trouble and we have no idea what to do for them or the strength to do it.

We read terrible statistics about the marriages that break up after the death of a child and we are disturbed. TCF's constant counsel of patience with one's self and then with others, as well as insights into other marriages that seem to be holding, works to reinforce the idea that a relationship may be basically okay in spite of the discovery that partners are not able to support each other while each is struggling to adapt to a crushing new reality.

In TCF we hear each other talk about how much it hurts, and all agree, and no one suggests any need to hurry it along or pretend the pain is gone. There will be someone there to say that it isn't quite as bad as it was, that it does get a little better after a while. Another nods.

There are difficulties on the job (or at home) of being disorganized, unable to concentrate or reach decisions. Lots of company there. It feels safe to discuss fears, dreams, anything. Through it all, we listen and respond. We take each other very seriously. We recognize each other's needs as our own, and those a little further along reach out to those coming on behind. It feels very good to be able to help someone else, and we recognize it as a sign of our own progress.

Some of us stay on, listening, reading, listening, attending conferences, listening—and learning. We have seen a lot of pain and a lot of healing. We have received much more than we have given. The Compassionate Friends works.

Ronnie Peterson
TCF, Star Lake, NY

DWELLING ON OUR LOSS

To an outsider, the idea of meeting with a group of people for the purpose of discussing death, our personal experiences with the death of our children, the "grief process," etc. may seem grim if not altogether morbid. All of us who are involved in The Compassionate Friends have run into someone who has asked, "Why do you do this?" or "Why don't you just try to let it go?" or "Why keep dwelling on the loss?"

The idea of "dwelling on the loss" is always stated with negative connotations; yet dwelling on the death of a child is not something we can avoid.

Indeed, "dwelling" is a part of the healing process; it's how we come to grips with the questions "Why, What if...?" that uncontrollably pop up in our minds. It is how we learn to accept the unacceptable.

Certainly there is a wealth of information in books dealing with death and dying. Our faith, our pastors, priests and rabbis have much to contribute to our healing. Psychologists, psychiatrists and therapy may be necessary. The Compassionate Friends encourages grieving parents to utilize any or all of the above tools, but we also realize the value of learning to verbalize openly, publicly, the grief and the loss we feel, not in the privacy of our doctors' or ministers' offices where we are very sheltered, but openly among people who know full well how hard it is to say "my child is dead." We do not put any pressure on the people attending our meeting to say anything. But the beautiful part of The Compassionate Friends' meeting is that it enables us to see people who are "down the long road" a way further and to realize that we will be there in time.

Are we dwelling on our loss? Absolutely; but we are learning to dwell on it constructively, to dwell on it without guilt and without the isolation that we all have felt. We learn how to bring our grief under control and how to reach out (in time) to others with a compassion that brings healing to others as well as ourselves.

Philip Barker
TCF, Sacramento, CA

CHAPTER III

IN THE BEGINNING

walking out of a long
and aching night—
wanting to be child and at home
wanting to feel warm

walking into a strange
and distant day—
wanting to weep and to sing
wanting to feel safe

walking along a dark
and haunted road—
wanting to find and be found
wanting to feel peace

Sascha

THE GRIEF PROCESS

CHANGE

The death of our child brings many changes to our lives and the lives of our families. The first change is death itself. Our child is dead—there is nothing we can do about that change. We mourn for this loss, saying "if only" and "why didn't we" as we struggle with acceptance of the finality of death.

Then the changes in our daily life stand out. The extra place at the table, our child's room, his possessions, his clothes, and the phone calls and letters that are no more. Each of us has experienced these agonizing and desperate changes—feeling helpless and frightened. Our anger and sense of unfairness over these changes can make our lives miserable, but we can do something about these changes. Once we realize nothing or no one can bring us peace but ourselves, we will begin to search for our personal peace. A person who needs, but refuses, the painful physical therapy exercise to correct an injury will remain a cripple for life. The same is true of emotional therapy. We must do some things that are painful at first if our emotional state is to become stable again. If we avoid all situations that might be painful, we may end up emotional cripples. Our progress is slow and very painful, but we can finally learn to use our grief in a positive way. Misery is optional - there is another way.

We have experienced not only death, but also life. Death has brought us closer to life and more aware of living. This awareness of living makes us aware of the needs of others. Our compassion is expanded, our understanding of life is changed and given time, we reach out to others in their time of need. We cannot cope with such a devastating loss and not be changed.

Betty Steigelmeyer
TCF, Colorado Springs, CO

A NEW SEASON

It is a new season; and there are new faces among us. Perhaps this is an ideal time to pause and reflect on grief.

Grief. What is it all about? Our child has died. We are unprepared. Part of our life is gone forever. It is final, irrevocable. Part of us is dead. We may feel numbness...denial...anger...panic...physical illness...guilt...depression. We learn that the divorce rate may be as high as 70% for families experiencing a child's death. (How indeed, can we communicate when a mere word reduces us to uncontrollable tears!) We long to run away from the pain and the memories. To sell the house. To move away. To start anew. Even making a decision is a major problem.

But wait. Our judgment is unsure. "Forgetting" is not the answer. We lose the ability to concentrate—bereaved parents do not function at their normal capacity. We find ourselves preoccupied. We make stupid mistakes in performing simple tasks at work, or at home. We wonder: "Am I losing my mind?"

No, this is grief.

Grief is very, very normal. Because we have loved, we grieve. There are no detours. There is no way around grief. We must work through our grief, so we may come to accept death as the final part of life, so we may learn to LIVE again.

First we must learn to live one day at a time.

Shirley Melin
TCF, Aurora, IL

IT ISN'T FAIR

It isn't fair (and there's a lot about life that isn't), but when a child dies, the responsiblity for maintaining relationships falls on the shoulders of those who are grieving. It seems it should be the other way around, doesn't it? Most of us expect those who love and care for us to be the ones who will understand our needs, reach out to us and support us while we struggle to regain some balance in our lives. So it comes as a rude shock when we discover some of these people don't understand our needs any more than the old proverbial man in the street. We become angry and disappointed.

It is a mistake for grieving people to try to make important decisions too early in their grief. In an effort to escape some of the pain, and because of the anger inherent in the situation, we often make decisions that seem right at the moment but, in fact, are not best for the long run. We sacrifice long-term pleasure for immediate gratification. Deciding who will and will not continue to be important and necessary in our lives from that time on certainly falls under the category of important decisions.

Think back now to the time before your child died. You must have known some bereaved people back there who were important to you. How well did you understand their feelings and needs? How good were you at being there for them through the long haul? Maybe you can remember feeling tongue-tied, inadequate and even cowardly, not because you didn't care, but because you cared so much that you couldn't cope with their pain. You felt inadequate, and so in their eyes you may have failed them, an assumption easy to make during the pain of fresh grief.

This is where the responsibility for relationships comes in. No important relationship should be severed during early bereavement without your having first made an effort to communicate your needs to those who love you. Before you cut people out of your life, at least try to educate them. Give them a book to read that spells out some of what you are going through and how they can best support you. Tell them how important they are to you and how much you need them to just be there and listen when you need to talk without having any answers for you. Impress upon them the fact that your grief for your child isn't going to be a short-term thing for you and ask for their patience, even if they don't understand.

Not everybody will be able to be there for you, no matter how hard you try to educate. If, however, you salvage one important relationship, it will have been worth your time and effort. Down the road a way, when you've had the necessary time to make your adjustment, you will find that some of these "unnecessary" people you gave up on too early in your grief really are a vital part of your life. It is difficult to go back and reestablish relationships that have been too long neglected.

No, it isn't fair, but we are the only ones who know how it feels to have been on both sides of the grief fence. Put that PhD you've earned the hard way to good use. The payoff comes later for you when you have regained some equilibrium in your life and you still have about you some of those who really do matter.

Mary Cleckley
TCF, Atlanta, GA

FALLING APART

I seem to be falling apart.
My attention span can be measured in seconds,
My patience in minutes.
I cry at the drop of a hat.
I forget things constantly.
The morning toast burns daily.
I forget to sign the checks.

Half of everything in the house is misplaced.
Anxiety and restlessness are my constant companions.
Rainy days seem extra dreary;
Sunny days seem an outrage.

Other people's pain and frustration seem
insignificant.
Laughing, happy people seem out of place in my
world.
It has become routine to feel half crazy.
I am normal, I am told.

I am a newly grieving person.

Eloise Cole
TCF, Phoenix, AR

THE GRIEF PROCESS

One out of one dies. Nothing, no one, lives forever. In an age of medical miracles, we have not yet eliminated death. Through technology we have introduced new and different choices concerning the when, where and how of death, but still not the whether. All things end at some point. Regardless of how much energy or emotional commitment we invest in a relationship, it cannot last forever. Because we care, because we invest a certain portion of ourselves into the cycles of others, we learn what it is to hurt and to grieve when those cycles are completed in one way or another.

If we have, then we are in danger of not having, and that loss (whether through death, divorce, abandonment or mutual dissolution) can be the most painful and devastating experience of our own cycles. Or it can be a point of growth and expansion of the spirit. But regardless, loss hurts.

Grief is a natural and normal reaction of loss, loss of any kind. It is a physical, emotional, spiritual and psychological response. The death of a child is perhaps the most devastating loss a person may experience. Yet grief occurs following any change in our lives. Even positive changes can bring a momentary grief response.

Grief is a complex process, guided by our past experiences, our religious beliefs, our socioeconomic situations, our physical health and the cause of the loss. Love, anger, fear, frustration, loneliness and guilt are all part of grief. It is important to understand that grief is not a sign of weakness or lack of faith. Grief is the price we pay for love.

In his research, Colin Murray Parkes identified four components of the grief process. When we first become aware of the loss, we become NUMB. Shock is a physiological phenomenon which protects us from further pain. When our circuits become overloaded, we cannot accept further information. We stop listening, stop hearing, and may feel like we've stopped breathing. A protective fog blankets us and cushions the reality of death. We switch to "automatic" and our responses become mechanical. Decisions are made, actions taken and events pass, all without our full participation. Shock is what helps us get through the necessary details of death. It can last anywhere from a few moments to several months.

When the shock or numbness wears off, the reality of our loss crashes into us. The collision with reality of death hurts. Parkes calls this part of the grief process "pining." We know it as HURT. Unlike the localized pain of a physical injury, this pain is totally engulfing. Every part of us hurts. There's a tightness in the throat, a searing pain in the chest, a heaviness in the heart. It hurts to move. It hurts to breathe. It hurts just to be! Sometimes the pain is so intense, we may develop physical symptoms. Sleep irregularities, changes in ap-

petite, and gastrointestinal disturbances are common. Heartache, restlessness, muscle tension and sighing may occur.

Anger and guilt are common emotions. We may feel angry with God, our spouses, our child or with others either involved with or totally separate from the death of our child. We may be angry with ourselves. Our sense of helplessness, intensifies our anger. WHY couldn't I prevent my child's death? "If only's" begin to haunt our thoughts. We trace over and over again the circumstances of our child's death, looking for something we should or could have done to prevent our child's death. WHY cries out, goes unanswered. Guilt feelings often accompany or follow anger. We may want to withdraw and be left alone.

Depression, feelings of emptiness and hollowness may temporarily overcome us. We may experience headaches, tightness in the throat or chest, muscle aches or a burning sensation in the stomach. GRIEF HURTS! We may, for awhile, become preoccupied with images of our child. We may "see" or sense our child's presence. We may begin to wonder if we are going crazy.

Parkes calls the next part of the grief process DEJECTION or DEPRESSION. Now pain is replaced by emptiness. It may seem as if we've fallen into a deep void. Apathy and deep depression are common. We may feel that our lives have lost all meaning. Who are we now that our child is dead? Am I still a mother if there is no child to kiss? Am I still a dad if there is no one to tuck in at night? How can we go on living when our child has died? We feel cheated, betrayed, robbed not only of our child's presence, but of our future as well.

As deep as the depression may become, other emotions can trigger a return to earlier feelings. Anger and guilt can be revisited many times during the grief process. We may begin to fear that we can never be happy again.

Does grief ever end? How can we possibly recover from the death of our child?

Parkes identifies the final phase of the grief process as RECOVERY. And yes indeed, recovery from the death of our child is possible! First, however, we must understand that grief takes far longer than most assume. One cannot recover from a child's death in a matter of weeks. It may take months or even years of traveling the roller coaster of emotions before recovery is achieved.

We can help ourselves through grief.

1. *Acknowledge the loss.*
2. *Accept the pain of grief. Try to live through it, not avoid it.*
3. *Share thoughts and feelings. Find enough compassionate listeners. We can talk more than one person can listen!*

4. Understand each person has an individual timetable for grief. Each person grieves separately and differently. We each move through grief at our own pace.
5. Find a sense of humor. Try to hang on to it.
6. Get some physical exercise. If nothing else, jog your memory.
7. Learn to hug again.
8. Accept yourself. Begin to understand you are someone new. Acknowledge that change.
9. Begin to become the person you already are.

Recovery from the death of a child is a matter of choice. Time does help heal over the open wounds. Scars form and serve as a reminder of battles once fought. Gradually, however, we must learn to live with those scars, and slowly they sink into place within the scheme of our lives.

Recovery is possible when we discover a smile flickering across our faces, when a chuckle grows into laughter and when memories bring warmth and comfort rather than tears and pain. Recovery begins to occur when we can learn to reinvest our energies, emotions and love rather than seek to replace them. We know we're making progress when we fully understand that putting our child's things away does not mean we are forgetting or negating his existence. When we completely understand we did not lose our child, recovery from grief is possible. Our child died, but the love we share between us can never be destroyed.

As we recover, we must learn who we are now and abandon attempts to return to who we used to be. A part, a big part, of us died when our child did. Yet, the sun got up the next morning and so did we. Our child died, we did not. Living continues. How it continues is up to us. We must learn to let go of the "what if's" and the "maybe's" and learn to dream new dreams.

Grief is the pulling of memories into focus. It is feeling, hurting, caring. It is struggling with the guilt that we might have done things differently or better and with the anger that we are left alone. Grief, in its pain and loneliness, is the memory of a loved one no longer here, but truly never far away.

Grief is the price we pay for love. We did not lose our children. They died, taking with them our hopes and dreams for the future, but never, never taking away their love. Though death comes, love will never go away. Hold it tight through the storms of grief and bring it into today.

LOVE NEVER GOES AWAY.

Darcie Sims
TCF - Albuquerque, NM

ANGER

Anger sometimes builds inside of me - even the hot coals of furious rage! If only I could take my fists and thrust blows at something, but then again, it will not really change my circumstances.

Does this all sound intimately familiar? Worse yet, do the overwhelming feelings manifest at the most unexpected times? While observing a mother pushing her child in a shopping cart in a market? While praying in church and catching glimpses of families who are all together? Then comes the subsequent feeling provoked by life's reality that some parents have been able to keep their children, while others have not. Yes, anger can be such a stabbing emotion that it can paralyze an ascent to the future.

Anger stems from hurt and we have been taught to control our tempers. How do we climb out of the conflict? First, recognize that it is normal and then express our feelings, in spurts, to a loved one or friend. Attend The Compassionate Friends' meetings, for those who have shared similar feelings can gather and bring comfort to one another. Repression of feelings can only lead to further depression, while expression, a necessary catharsis, vents pent-up emotions and shines a ray of light on a saddened and darkened spirit.

Floryana Walker
TCF, Lower Cape Cod

WHY ANGER?

What makes us the most angry?

- *Anger at those who don't want to talk about or listen to us talk about the dead child*
- *Anger because home doesn't feel like home anymore since the child's death*
- *Anger because we're never happy anymore or never have any fun anymore*
- *Anger at people who fail to realize the depth of our loss*
- *Anger at seeing children the same age as our dead children or the same age our child would have been had they not died*
- *Anger at our helplessness and frustration over the situation*
- *Anger at those who say the wrong things, or worse, those who say nothing*
- *Anger because life is going on for everyone but us*
- *Anger because nothing will ever be the same again*
- *Anger at financial difficulties from the child's death*
- *Anger at other parents who don't appreciate their own good fortune*
- *Anger at well-meaning friends who say that all we need is to "get involved in something new" or to "stay busy"*
- *Anger because religion doesn't help, and anger because we feel that way*
- *Anger because we have been "singled out" for tragedy and disaster*
- *Anger because our spouse is never grieving the same way we are*
- *Anger at the doctors or others who we feel could have saved our child*
- *Anger and impatience with others who complain about things that seem so petty compared to the death of a child*
- *Anger when other parents neglect or abuse their children*
- *Anger at the perpetrators if death was a homicide or car accident*
- *Anger at our judicial system and the inefficiences of police departments*
- *Anger at doctors for not preparing parents for the child's imminent death*
- *Anger toward doctor who treated the child (if suicide victim) and didn't notice degree of depression; and anger toward ourselves for not noticing that child was suicidal*
- *Anger that it always seems to be the best kids who die*
- *Anger at the insensitivities and lack of personal touch of the doctors*

- Anger at the child for not being careful
- Anger at seeing friends' kids receive honors, graduate, get married, etc. when our children never will
- Anger at ourselves when we have a good time
- Anger at ourselves when we are angry

How can we express our anger in a healthy manner? Some suggestions:

- Screaming in a private place, like a closed car, into the wind, or the woods
- Kicking a can down the street or in the basement
- Beating the floor with a towel or pillow
- Beating the bed with a tennis racquet or shoe
- Smashing bricks with a bat or hammer
- Throwing books or shoes, ripping magazine or newspapers
- Splitting wood or pounding nails
- Target or skeet shooting
- Buying old dishes at garage sales and then smashing them
- Tiring housework like window washing, wax stripping, garage cleaning
- Jogging, swimming, and running
- Just plain crying
- Sometimes distractions like novels or movies help dissipate rage. If concentration is a problem, read short stories or articles or watch TV
- Telling others around us about our anger - if nothing else, it may educate
- Calling child's name aloud in private places
- Screaming or yelling about the perpetrator (if applicable)

You may notice that most of these activities are physical. You may feel drained afterwards, but you will feel better.

Houston West Chapter -TCF

LET'S TALK ABOUT ANGER

Your child has died, and on top of all the other new and different feelings that are now a part of your being, you find that anger, too, has reared its head. It isn't hard to find targets at which to direct your anger. They're all around, conveniently waiting for you to single them out. There's nothing strange about this for, you see, anger is a large part of the grief process for many.

Anger isn't considered a good emotion. Many have been programmed from early childhood not to show anger. "Don't you raise your voice to me, young lady, (or stamp your foot, or slam that door)!" As a result, it is difficult for these people to even admit that they are angry, and that somebody must pay! Many will deny this emotion in the groups, but the seasoned, sharing bereaved parent can often sense the rage within those parents and with gentle probing and reassurance, can help a parent to identify what they're really feeling and that it's really okay to feel that way.

Anger isn't an emotion that just goes away if not admitted. It simply buries itself in the sands of your being. There it festers and gnaws until you become an ugly, twisted person who is no longer able to have satisfactory relationships with yourself, much less with others.

The healthy way to deal with anger is to admit it, first off, and to know that you're not a bad person because you are angry. The second thing is to identify why you are angry, and the truth of that is you're really angry because your child is dead (and that's more than a good enough reason). Third, you need to recognize those who are the targets of your anger. You may find yourself angry with people who just happened to be convenient. For instance: the doctor or nurse who showed no obvious compassion at the time of the death; the emergency medical people who didn't get there fast enough, you think; The Compassionate Friends organization if, for example, you felt in the beginning that your grief was private and you saw our efforts to extend a helping hand as an intrusion, or maybe we spelled your name wrong; the people around you who you thought would know the right things to say or do to ease your pain, but who failed you instead because they didn't understand your needs; or your spouse because he or she can't make it better and is grieving totally differently from you (maybe even demanding that you do it his way), or because there was buried anger within your relationship with your spouse from things or situations that had nothing to do with your child's death, but is now surfacing.

If there was a suicide involved, it's easy to blame your child's spouse or girl or boyfriend. "If only they had treated him better," you think.

The anger - no rage - that comes from the fact that your child was murdered. The knowing that someone deliberately took your child's life; no accident here. It was intentional. That's an anger that is more easily understood and there's no problem identifying it. Besides the murderer, there are also convenient targets of law enforcement people who do their jobs poorly, you think, or the opposing attorneys who try to make your dead child the culprit. If your child was killed by a drunk driver, you have many of the same targets as one whose child was murdered. Often the offender is merely slapped on the wrist, or if he was also killed in the wreck, though he has received the ultimate punishment, you still may feel frustrated that you were denied his day in court.

Maybe you see your God at fault because your child is dead. Do you feel He failed you and are you angry about that? Have you admitted that to Him and felt free to wrestle with it?

The list could go on and on. I am sure you have several targets of your own to add to the list. We find many outlets for anger which is better, some say, than blaming yourself totally and living with the depression of that. The important thing is to admit the anger that is inherent in the situation and get it out in the open. Bring it to TCF meetings and talk about it, or share it with a trusted friend who may not understand it, but who can hear it without making you feel guilty for being angry.

Sometimes there are things you can do to help you express and then let go of this anger. Some people find it can be dispelled by telling the person, either face to face or by letter, just why you are angry. Some letters need only be written and never mailed for often it is the act of expressing your frustration that allows you to let go of it. If your child died a violent death and from your experiences you see a need for changes in our laws and system, it can be a tremendous help to work for these changes and have something meaningful occur because of your anger. Nobody in TCF says you shouldn't be angry. Instead, they encourage you to admit, identify, recognize, express, knowing that you may not be able to let go of it right now. You are encouraged, however, to have a goal of doing what is necessary to express and dispel it and reach out toward the time when you can let go of the anger. As long as you choose to be angry, know that you are denying yourself any pleasure that is left out there for you, for anger and happiness do not walk hand in hand. You have been hurt enough, you deserve whatever happiness you can find, and there is some. Make letting go of anger your goal and start today working toward it. It is a kind thing that you do for yourself - and you do deserve kind things.

Mary Cleckley
TCF, Atlanta, GA

GUILT

GUILT: HOW TO CONQUER IT

Few people escape some feelings of guilt when a loved one dies, whether the loved one died as the result of something totally outside of the griever's control, or as the result of an accident in which the griever was directly involved. We seem to feel that somehow we could have prevented our loved one's death whether in reality we could have prevented it or not. Guilt can create a considerable amount of difficulty for the grieving person, and if it is not resolved, it can prevent healthy resolution of grief.

There are various types of guilt. They are: causation guilt, cultural guilt, moral guilt, survival guilt, and recovery guilt. While we label the different types, it is important to remember that rarely are our guilt feelings brought about by only one type of guilt, but a combination of the various types.

With causal guilt, we believe that something we did or did not do caused the death. Persons with this kind of guilt will say: "I should have insisted she see the doctor sooner" or "I should have seen that he was depressed."

Cultural guilt comes from cultural expectations. In our society a "good" wife sees that her husband takes proper care of his health. A "good" son or daughter cares for and protects his/her aging parent. When the person who has died was a child or a young adult, grieving parents are even more likely to feel this guilt because of the myth that, as parents, we should protect our children at all costs.

Moral guilt comes from fantasies related to sin and punishment. It is the idea that our loved one's death is a punishment for some sin that we have committed in our past. With this guilt you will hear, "I tried to be a good person; why did this happen to me?" or "I know this is a punishment for . . ." While our religious faith may not actually state that we will be punished for our sins in this world, we assume that this is what is meant and see our loved one's death as our punishment.

Survival guilt is another type. Older bereaved people are especially susceptible to survival guilt. They ask, "Why am I still living at sixty or seventy, and this younger person is dead?" They feel guilty that they have lived the number of years they have and have experienced much more of life than the deceased did. Bereaved grandparents are very likely to experience survival guilt.

The last type of guilt is recovery guilt. This sets in when we have a not so painful day or begin to recover. We think we are being disloyal to our loved one if we are not continuing to suffer.

Guilt can be conscious or unconscious. Unconscious guilt is the most difficult to deal with because we are not directly aware that we feel guilt. A manifestation of unconscious guilt can be seen in defensiveness at talk of the cause of the deceased's death. Frequently this is the case when the death occurred under circumstances such as a suicide or an accident involving the deceased's use of drugs or alcohol.

Projection is another way unconscious guilt can manifest itself. Projection is when we put the blame onto someone else rather than ourselves. We blame the doctor for not doing enough, instead of recognizing that we feel guilty that we did not get our loved one to the doctor soon enough.

Unconscious guilt is not only difficult to rid ourselves of because we are not directly aware of it, but it is the most destructive. It may lead us to destructive behavior such as alcoholism or drug abuse, working until we drop, engaging in demeaning activities or work, or by constantly subjecting ourselves to the demands of others. These behaviors are a way of unconsciously saying, "I am guilty; therefore, I am unworthy and should be punished."

To rid ourselves of guilt we must first be aware that we "feel" guilty. Then we must identify, as clearly as possible, just what it is we believe we are guilty of. The next step is to ask ourselves if the guilt is logical or not. A good way of doing this is to ask ourselves: "With the information and resources I had at the time, did I do the best I could?" Ask yourself specific questions, such as "Did I know her depression was so deep that she was even thinking of taking her own life?" or "Did I know when I let him take the car that night he was going to have an accident?" These questions appear ridiculous with their obvious answers, but these questions help us to look at our guilt in its true light. Another thing to consider when looking at our guilt is what was our intention when we made the decision or action that we did. Obviously we did not intend that the results would be as they were. The real value in examining our guilt in a logical way is that it gives us a different perspective from which to view our actions.

It takes time to resolve guilt, and one time of logical examination will not do it. It must be done over and over again. Talking with a nonjudgmental person about our guilt is helpful. Many times when we say our guilts out loud, we can hear the illogic of them. Writing out guilt feelings in a journal or in a letter to the deceased helps many people. Imagining ourselves talking directly to our loved one is another way to deal with guilt. Some people find it is helpful to simply wallow in their guilt for a period of time until they tire of it.

A sudden death offers a better chance for guilt since the death freezes the relationship. What is said or done at the last parting is crucial. We get "hooked" into guilt because we play over and over in our minds the bad parts of the scene. Try instead to play the whole scene - one complete with both the good and bad parts.

For some grievers, asking for forgiveness from our loved one or God is the only answer. Most important is forgiving yourself. Confession may be helpful for those who are Catholic. For those of other faiths, a talk with your clergyperson may bring forgiveness.

However you resolve your guilt, whether by looking at it logically or by seeking forgiveness, it is important that you make every attempt to do it. Know that you cannot live the rest of your life punishing yourself over something that cannot be changed. You have suffered enough.

Margaret Gerner, M.S.W.
TCF, St. Louis, MO

IF ONLY

"If only" is the whip with which we lash ourselves.
If only I had not bought him a motorcycle . . .
If only I had not let her cross the street alone . . .
If only I had forbidden him to drive while he was so tired . . .
If only I had not permitted the surgery . . .
If only I had allowed the surgery sooner . . .
If only I had not waited for the ambulance . . .
If only I had waited for trained personnel to move her . . .
If only I were an all-knowing, all-powerful God,
I would not have allowed my child to die.
But I am only human.

Theresa Hutchison
TCF, Norman, OK

DEALING WITH HEALING

Guilt: A feeling of culpability for offenses. (Webster)

Grief is a process that naturally sets us up for guilt and self-blame; it's common. You perceive a discrepancy between what was done and what should have been done.

Some of the things that can lead a parent to feel guilt after the death of a child:

1. *Not getting the child to the doctor in time.*
2. *"If I hadn't let him/her have the car that day..."*
3. *Grandiose sense of power. (Parents feel they can control all things that happen to their children. They can't.)*
4. *Acts of ommission or commission.*
5. *Unfinished business with dead child.*
6. *Feelings of unintentional negligence.*
7. *Defective genes.*
8. *Being angry with God.*
9. *Being angry with dead child.*
10. *Not wanting unborn child, negative feelings about pregnancy.*
11. *Lack of companionship, regrets regarding this; parent/child relationships, communication, "If Onlys," regrets during life, lack of display of affection.*
12. *Misleading guidance.*
13. *Causative guilt (magical thinking) - something that you feel you somehow did that led to the death.*
14. *Guilt over punishment or discipline.*
15. *Joy in your own recovery.*
16. *Being unable to help child face death.*

Things that might help you deal with guilt:

1. *Face the event honestly.*
2. *Eat well, exercise, stay busy.*
3. *It is normal to feel guilty; it's okay. Believe this.*
4. *Concentrate on the positive aspects of your life with the child.*
5. *Participate in self-help groups. TCF works; I've seen it.*
6. *Ignore insensitive remarks. If you just can't tell the person how you feel about what they have said, be as nice as you can be; you are educating them.*
7. *Seek counseling if you feel you need it. It's no sin or disgrace to need professional help; you have experienced the most devastating blow a parent can experience.*
8. *Find someone who will "be there." You need a friend now more than ever in your life.*
9. *Believe in yourself. You are a good person; you did the very best you could under the circumstances.*
10. *Believe God loves you, that he understands. He will forgive you. He knows how you feel; He is a bereaved parent too. He can take your anger. You probably judge yourself more harshly than He judges you.*
11. *Be kind to yourself; you've been punished enough already.*
12. *Be patient with yourself. In time you will heal.*
13. *Talk, talk, talk about your child and his/her death. Talk until you have talked it out.*
14. *Look for hope and signs of it. It's there, in people, flowers, everywhere.*

Fay Harden
TCF, Tuscaloosa, AL

NEWLY BEREAVED PARENTS

MISSING YOU

I just can't believe it . . .
The sun still rises and sets,
The moon and stars still shine,
The flowers still bloom,
The birds still sing.
I expected a change
In everything.

I just can't believe it . . .
It still gets dark and light,
The ocean still has waves,
The rain still rains,
The wind still blows.
Is it because
They do not know?

I just can't believe it . . .
I thought the world would stop
When in my house I found
An empty chair,
A missing smile.
I thought it would stop
For just awhile.

I just can't believe it . . .

Greta Viney
TCF, Yakima, WA

GRIEF

GRIEF is sometimes silent - like snowflakes falling on a dark winter's night - but never peaceful or serene or pretty like the pure white snow. When grief is silent, the tears seem to turn to ice, like the snowflakes, before they reach our eyes.

GRIEF is sometimes raging - like a monstrous thunderstorm - with all its fury and bolts of lightning striking our hearts at every angle. When grief is raging, the tears come in torrents like the rain and flood our soul.

GRIEF: Whether it be silent or raging . . . HURTS.

Verna Smith
FCF, Ft. Worth, TX

TAKE YOUR TIME

The one phrase we hear more than any other is "It'll take time for you to get over your child's death." We know that this is spoken with care and love. But little do we know at the beginning of our grief just what time means: the first time, the day time, the night time, the last time, all of these times. The one thing we can say is "take it." Take all the time you need. Grief is hard work, and we need to take the time for all of the aspects we talk so much about to really work through it.

Take the time to feel; it's hard but worth it. We can't just push those feelings aside because they are part of who we are, how we've managed, and the life we've had. All of our life experiences combine to affect our feelings.

Take the time to talk. Talk to anyone who seems to care about you. Ask your friends and family if they will take the time to listen. If you need a telephone listener, call the National Office or one of the local chapter listeners. They have time to listen.

Take the time to read. When you read the experiences of others, you will realize that you're not alone. Maybe a special book will help you understand what is happening to you during this time we call bereavement. Take the time to read and reread the paragraphs or chapters that help.

Take the time to physically care for yourself. If you like to walk, jog, or run, go out and use that time to help you feel better. Get enough rest; take the time to sleep late some days, or go to bed earlier if you need to. Sleeping may be an escape but if it helps you, take the time for a extra few hours. Take care of yourself by eating better. Try to understand that food gives you some energy and that food helps satisfy unmet needs. Food is always better for you than drugs or alcohol, and a small weight gain or loss is not unusual. Take the time to understand what is happening to your body.

Take the time to be angry or guilty without letting these feelings ruin your life. You may think your life is ruined anyhow and who cares, but anger and guilt turned inward can destroy your self-esteem faster than anything. Take time to sort through these feelings, acknowledge them, and then let them go.

Know that when someone says "It'll take time," we can nod and try to accept that as part of our getting through these days, months, years.

Remember that someday you will take the time to help someone else and that time will be the most satisfying time of all.

Therese Goodrich
Executive Director
National Office

CONTROL

The pain we feel is almost constant for many months, but there are times when it completely overwhelms us. At these times we can do nothing but pace and wait. We wring our hands. Our bodies tremble with agony and despair. We feel regret, wishing to the depth of our souls that we could redo the yesterday when our child died. We feel intense longing for our child, so intense we don't believe we can stand it for another minute. We feel completely alone. It is as though no one exists in this world but us. Between sobs, phrases like "My God, I can't go on" or "It hurts so badly" come out of our mouths over and over again. We feel as though we are at the bottom of a deep pit and there is no way out. We feel consumed with an indescribable anguish.

It is at these times we might be advised by those around us to "calm down" or to "control ourselves." It is my opinion that is exactly what we should not do. I mistakenly tried to "control" my emotions after Arthur died, but when I could "control" no longer, my grief would pour out of me in a raging torrent. I noticed that for days after one of these sessions I felt a great release of pressure, but never did realize that these wailing sessions were helpful and healing.

Every emotion carries with it energy. Sadness, anger, guilt, regret are with us constantly in our grief, but the energy caused by them cannot be released as it builds. It is like a tea kettle. The water is constantly boiling, but it is in spurts that the steam pushes itself out the lid. The uncontrolled crying session is the steam of our boiling emotions forcing itself out. As with the lid on the tea kettle, these sessions are our safety valves.

These sessions can last from a few minutes to over an hour. They are self-terminating and they are exhausting. After such a session we are worn out just as we would be after hard physical exercise. Sometimes we can even sleep after them. Early in our grief they may be frequent, but as time goes on and you allow yourself to experience them and not try to inhibit them, they will become farther apart.

Don't take the advice of those around you to "get hold of yourself." On the contrary, surrender yourself to your pain. Cry. Wail. Rant. Wring your hands. Voice your anger, your guilts, your regrets. Expend your pent-up emotions. You will feel much better afterwards.

Margaret Gerner
TCF, St. Louis

THE MAGIC OF YOU

"What can I do to get better?" This is the question most often asked by newly bereaved parents, as if the right actions could work a miracle. They are seeking easy rules, methods, or steps of healing.

But there are none. There are no special words, no miraculous system, no magic wand to take the pain away. There is only time, hard work, and compassionate support. Grief is a process which must be allowed to function thoroughly in order for healing to take place. There are no shortcuts. Attempts to ease the process—such as through alcohol or drugs—often end either in disaster or in complicating the process.

There is no magic. There is only you, the bereaved person, who must decide yourself to work within the process to resolve your grief. No one else can do it for you, but others can help by supporting your grief rather than searching for magic words to wish it away. Others can help within The Compassionate Friends by providing models of healed parents who are willing to listen and to share.

You can help yourself by being patient with grief instead of searching for easy methods. You can help yourself by learning about the grief process. You can help yourself by sharing your story with others and by listening to their stories. You can help yourself by reaching out to others, for helping others is the source of your own healing.

Magic pills, wands, or incantations? There are none. Look to yourself. The Compassionate Friends can help, but you alone determine the progress of your grief. The magic of healing is within you.

Marcia Alig
TCF, Mercer Area Chapter, NJ

TEARS HAVE TEMPERATURES

Scalding hot - Overwhelmed with pain and sorrow, the "I can't believe it" tears.
Burning hot - Grief that knows no bounds and no future.
Warm - A relief to let go some of the hurt and sadness.
Cool - Your emotions are on "hold," but your control is slack.
Cold - Your insides feel empty and the pain has no direction.

Yes, tears have temperatures:
I know this is true.
I have cried them all.

And I bet you have too.

Shirley Blakely Curle
TCF, Little Rock, AR

WHY ARE THERE SATURDAYS?

Why are there Saturdays?
These are the days when there
is no routine.
It used to be my day for
catching up,
For doing chores or resting for
the week ahead.

Why are there Saturdays?
These are the days when your
brother and sister
Go off to visit their father
and leave me alone
With the whispers of the child
that no longer lives.

Why are there Saturdays?
These are the days when I
see your smile
In the wagging tail of your
devoted dog
As she searches the house for you
one more time
And settles down for a nap
under your old bed.

Why are there Saturdays?
These are the days that I
look for you.
Sitting on the bench as I
watch your twin play basketball
I search every face for those
sparkling brown eyes
And watch every step taken
for your loping gait.

Why are there Saturdays?
These are the days when there
is no routine.
I use them as my days for
catching up
For the tears that will not come
on any other day
But swell under my breast
until they flow down my face

On Saturday.

Georgiann Bertrand
TCF, Bluegrass Chapter, KY

HOW MANY CHILDREN DO YOU HAVE?

The question about the number of children you have usually falls into the category of small talk. Very often it is the equivalent of "How are you?" In both cases, seldom is the inquirer interested in the answer to either question. These type questions do help fill in awkward spots in conversations with people you don't know very well. Before your child dies, you attach no importance to it, but once the death occurs, that question takes on tremendous significance.

Shortly after the death of my son, I realized that the question about the number of children I had was going to be bothersome. Each time someone asked, I struggled with the answer. I soon decided I was not going to let this become a problem. I thought about how I felt about my choices of answers and chose the one that met my needs when my grief was fresh. I had a surviving daughter, but I knew for me to answer "One" would seem a denial on my part that my son had lived, and that wasn't right for me. So in the beginning when I still needed to tell people that my son had died, I would answer the question in detail about my son and his accident. As the months passed, I found that it wasn't necessary any longer to go into detail every time the question came my way. My needs had changed, so I re-thought my answer.

Now when I am asked how many children I have, I answer "I had two children." The criterion I use in determining if I go any further is whether or not the person asking is going to be a continuing part of my life. If so, they need to know about my son, and I tell them; otherwise, it could cause problems in the relationship if we dance around the truth of the matter.

If, on the other hand, the person asking is simply passing through my life, then I feel no need to go any further than "I had two children." Seldom does anyone catch the had instead of have and pursue it. If they do and ask follow-up questions about ages and professions, I tell them first that my 26-year-old son was killed in an accident and then I tell them about my daughter who is alive and well. They can either acknowledge my son's death and ask questions, or they can ignore him completely and ask about my daughter. I am comfortable either way. If they are embarrassed, I see that as their problem. Just to show you how different we all are, however, my husband feels comfortable answering "We have one child." That is what is right for him and that is what he should say.

You can eliminate the agony of trying to decide each time how you should answer this question. All you need do is sit down right now and decide on the answer that is right for you at this point in your grief - then say it. When your needs change, so can your answer. By doing this, you defuse that powerful question and it loses its ability to traumatize.

Mary Cleckley
TCF, Atlanta,GA

BACK INTO THE WORLD

There would always come those moments when a bright red top found under the lilac, a snatch of tune, a small mitten at the back of a closet, a child's footprint in the soft earth of the back yard would cut into me, sweeping Teddy back with terrible force,and I would go down into the basement and sit on one of the sawhorses and give way to long shuddering sobs, until the seizure finally wore itself out and let me go again. And then I would wipe my face and climb back upstairs again, where the world - impossibly, capriciously - was going along exactly as it had before.

Anton Myrer
The Last Convertible

Like the character in Anton Myrer's novel, all of us have had the experience of having to pull ourselves together in order to face the things that seem to continue in spite of our every wish for them to stop. I remember going back to work, sitting at my desk and staring blankly at the walls. The people I worked with struggled to say the right things, but they continued, also, to do the same things they always did. And I guess I wished or expected or wanted something to be different, because my world had changed so drastically in the days I had been gone.

I remember seeing my friends again. And they were kind and brought food or said they were sorry, or they hugged me and maybe cried with me. But they were still the same friends, eating the same foods and reading the same books; and I guess I thought they would change, for certainly I had changed since I had last seen them.

And the news on TV and the time of year and the color of the sky and everything else must surely change, but it didn't and it doesn't and the world "impossibly, capriciously" continues just as it always has.

The death of a child has probably changed each of us more than any single other event in our lives. And the world seems cruel sometimes to not allow us the time to adjust and catch up.

But no amount of hoping will stop the goings-on around us. Slowly, strongly and eventually, we must make the effort, on our own, to catch up.

Gerald Hunt
TCF, White River Junction, Vermont

CHAPTER IV

THE WHOLE FAMILY GRIEVES

we who were left behind
to know the shadows
we who were left behind
to touch the night
we who were left behind
to heal the darkness and
to share this day

we who have turned once more
to hope and loving
though we were given graves
and lifeless children —
we hear them now
these children and their song
reminding us
reminding us again
that we must fill the time
we spend in life
with understanding
tenderness and peace

Sascha

THE GRIEF OF MOTHERS

SITTING HERE

To sit here and not think of you is
impossible.
To sit here and not be able to touch
you is unbearable.
To sit here and not be able to hear
your voice is torture.
To sit here and not be able to watch
you play outside with your brother
is pure agony.
To sit here and watch your brother
play alone hurts.
To sit here and watch your daddy and
brother play together and see that
certain look in their eyes that says,
"We wish you were here," makes
my heart ache.
But to be able to sit here and
remember your smile, your touch,
hearing your voice, thinking of the
times you did play outside with
your brother, thinking of the times
you did play with daddy and
brother, and thinking of the times
I'd kneel beside your bed as you
slept and cry a tear because I loved
you so, are pure heaven.
Because no one can ever take my
memories away,
To sit here and be with you in my
heart is truly a wonderful time in
my day.
To sit here...

Nancy Barrs
TCF, Salinas, CA

MEMORIAL DAY

I saw you today, in the downy soft face of a newborn babe, nestled lovingly in the protective arms of his mom. I felt the joy that only a mother could feel, radiating from her face as she proudly gazed at him. It took me back to another day when you first came into my life.

I saw you today in a precocious four-year-old at the supermarket. His little hands grabbed for colorful boxes of cereal and other goodies. His bewildered young mom kept one hand on him and one on the cart while explaining to him why he couldn't have everything he saw and what would happen to him if he didn't behave.

I heard your voice today through the backyard fence in the voices of children as they negotiated at play. Who was going to be the first to go down the slide and who was going to tell Timmy next door that he couldn't play? My mind raced back to another day when you came running in from play, saying someone wasn't being fair. I wiped the tears from your dark little face and brushed your hair back with my hand. Somehow a hug and a kiss would even the score. Out you'd go, to get into it again.

I saw you today, in a young boy 12 or 13 years old racing his bike down the street. I remember the blue one we bought for you and how proud you were of it. How I worried as you flew like the wind down the street, hoping you wouldn't get hit by some careless driver; how we searched the town after it was stolen from the parking lot at school; the disappointment you felt when we couldn't find it.

I saw you today on the football field as the boys were out for practice. Driving by, I remembered your games, the ones I missed because I had to work. How proud I was when I did see you play, remembering your enthusiasm, how you wanted that scholarship.

I saw you today in a young army private just home on leave; those civilian clothes were no cover for that short cropped hair. Your hair, soft as a kitten it was. I was the only one you'd trust to cut it. "Thanks, Mom," you'd say, "that's just how I wanted it." That hair, cut within an inch of your scalp, was not at all your style. You looked so strange this Christmas when you came home on leave. But you were my son, and you looked very handsome to me, and I was so very proud of you.

I saw you today in the handsome strong face of an eighteen-year-old. The smile on his face belied the turmoil within. Only God knows why he, like you, decided that life wasn't worth living anymore. He ended his life with a single shot just as you ended yours. I sit and stare at his picture in the obituary column of the morning paper. Hot tears sting my face as I think of his mom, how much she must have loved him. I share in her grief, remembering the numbness of the first few days, the unbearable pain. I say a silent prayer for her and the young man, knowing for her what surely lies ahead. As she lays her son to rest, her memorial day has just begun. For as each passing moment, hour, and day evolve into weeks, months and years, she will see her son and hear his voice in someone else's child, and she will remember.

Mary A. Bell
TCF, Ankeny, IA

SOFTLY ON MY MIND

Softly on my mind,
Ever caressing my memory,
A child that is still part of me,
the child of my heart.

You say he is dead.
I know he is very much alive.
Laughing brown eyes,
A sweet soft voice,
I still see his eyes light with mischief.
I still hear his voice.
Oh, don't tell me he is dead,
When in my heart he lives.

What I have is memory,
The mind's blurring pictures,
A mother's love beyond time,
An ache to hold my child again.
I remember now his smile.
Other times I hear his cry.
Sometimes it is just a flicker;
And now he is part of my heart,
Resting softly on my mind.

Edie Kaplan
TCF, West Broward/Ft. Lauderdale FL

A TEAR FELL

I rode by your school by chance today
And I just happened to look that way.
The boys all had their ball caps on;
then I remembered my son was gone.
Just when I thought I was doing so well,
Before I knew it - a tear fell.
Then on Sunday as I sat in church
I looked around and missed you so much.
I saw other boys in their Sunday suits
And I remembered you were just as cute.
People all think I'm doing so well;
They don't know today - a tear fell.
When I'm reminded of what might have been
It gets too hard to hold it in.
When life will catch me off my guard,
That's when I seem to be hit so hard.
It seems all roads lead back to you
As I take each day and try to get through.
They say time makes it better, but I cannot tell;
I only know today - a tear fell.

Carolyn Bryan
TCF, Orange Park, FL

JENNY

No longer a reason to waken.
Nothing to make rising worthwhile.
Gone is the light, the warmth
of Jenny's morning smile.

Sunshine always filled the room,
Whether skies were gray or blue.
The brightness came from Jenny's smile—
Her eyes and laughter, too.

Jenny, with the morning smile
of love upon your face—
Each wakening was a precious gift—
To have you one more day.

I wish that it were yesterday;
Today came much too soon.
If it could be yesterday,
I would still have you.

Carole Hughes
TCF, Tulsa, OK

URGENT

Nothing is urgent anymore.
No blinking lights
No beepers beeping
No cars screeching.
There are no red flags skipping
  up and down on slippery
  car-crash roads.

When David died
  all the lights went out
And jumped up
  into the sky with David.

Call the fireman if you smell smoke
Dial ambulance if you see a flood of
  blood
Phone me if Grandma dies...
But please don't scream URGENT!

When David died
  all the lights went out
And nothing is urgent anymore.

Nancy Jansen
TCF, Cape Cod, MA

THE GRIEF OF FATHERS

STRENGTH

In the early days of my grief,
a tear would well up in my eyes,
a lump would form in my throat,
but you would not know -
I would hide it,
And I am strong.

In the middle days of my grief,
I would look ahead and see that wall
that I had attempted to go around
as an ever-present reminder of a wall
yet unscaled.
Yet I did not attempt to scale it
for the strong will survive -
And I am strong.

In the later days of my grief,
I learned to climb over that wall -
step by step -
remembering, crying, grieving.
And the tears flowed steadily
as I painstakingly went over.
The way was long, but I did make it,
For I am strong.

Near the resolution of my grief,
a tear will well up in my eyes,
a lump will form in my throat,
but I will let that tear fall -
and you will see it.
Through it you will see
that I still hurt and I care,
For I am strong.

Terry Jago
TCF, Regina, Canada

THERE IS A ROOM

There is a room in our home whose door is closed.
I open it from time to time and pause awhile.
The red carpet is somewhat stained,
  an old spill, perhaps.
Hair oils darken the wall
  beside where the bed once stood.
A candy wrapper, a popcorn kernel or two,
  lie beside the roller skates.
All of this hid in the dark beneath the bed.
Now the bed is gone, as are most of the clothes.
Dressers stand alone around the desk,
  drawers full, cluttered with mementos.
The closet holds a few tools, a batter's cap,
  a down vest, a fishing pole.
It is Olin's room.
Here he lives in memory only.
I stand quietly
  and remember waking him up in the morning,
  starting a day.
Within these walls we talked a lot,
  sometimes in anger, often with love.
In here I cared for him when he was sick.
Sometimes we'd wrestle, laugh,
  look at papers, see a drawing.
In this place I held him in my arms,
  dried his tears, kissed him good night.
There were hard moments, too, within these walls.
They have heard arguments, lectures,
  seen him placed across my knee.
But mostly they witnessed hugs and closeness,
  caring and love.
In this room I hear the whispers of our yesterday
and know I love him still.

Someday this room will be a den, but not too soon.
I've taken care of some furniture, but not all.
Some things have been discarded, but not too much.
A few things have been stored away,
but there's a lot to go.
There is still much to do,
transforming this part of my past.
It's like my soul: a little cluttered,
a bit dirty, just partially picked up.
In its slow transformation back to life
I say my good-byes.
Mostly, though, I watch my now,
blessed and built in countless memories,
Unfold to the future.

Don Hackett
TCF, South Shore, Boston, MA

KATHY'S DAY

George Washington was a special person to our nation. So, too, were Christopher Columbus, Abraham Lincoln and Martin Luther King.

In our country, we recognize these and other special people with specific days set aside for us to honor their lives and memories. Official events are held, and most of us usually do something different from our daily routine. Often we do something extra special and traditional.

Within a few years after Kathy's death, I decided that I would set aside a special day to honor her life and memory. I chose the anniversary of her death. It was a day I already would be thinking about her in a special way. Over the years, the day has acquired a certain tradition.

If it is a work day, I take the day off. In the morning, I visit her grave and talk to her - kind of bring her up to date on what has happened and what I am doing. Then for the rest of the day, I do something special. One year I went to the seashore and walked on the beach. Other years I have gone to a museum or art gallery. When I was single, I usually was alone - now my wife (even though she never knew Kathy) joins me. We celebrate Kathy's life and memory. I don't expect the world to join in this celebration, but neither will I let the year be complete without this special day being included in the calendar of hearts.

Bill Ermatinger
TCF, Baltimore, MD

EVEN WHEN WE ARE APART

"Even when we are apart, I am still with you." These words still make me cry. I read them on a Father's Day card that Elaine got for me after Sean died. I cherish these words and keep that card safely tucked away. It is difficult for me to explain the deep feelings I associate with these words. Is Sean indeed still with me? He is certainly still in my heart.

I always wanted to be a father that Sean would be proud of. I know that I consciously make decisions based on how they would look through Sean's eyes. I still want Sean to be proud of me.

I don't feel any psychic link to Sean, although I wish I did. I do feel he is aware of my actions. I hope wherever he is, he is able to say, "That's my Dad," with a proud smile in his heart.

Sean is still with me and I am with him. We will be forever linked, no matter how far apart. Our hearts are together.

Tom Spray
TCF, Simi Valley, CA

LEGACY

Eyelashes, whiskers, thread—
Yours, mine, his and hers—
Defy vacuum, broom and rag.
They divide to spread
Family investment.

Our boy lives here still.
An odd twist of dust
In the baseboard slot,
Blue crayon on the cellar stair
Are parts of him.

A long dent in the mattress,
Paint scabs on the sill,
the chip on the mower blade —
Fragments of a lively tune
That dances him around us.

Nail holes, oil spots
Stare at us.
The door he bent one autumn
Still lets flies in, heat out.
His song hums in every room.

R. C. Purdy
TCF, York, PA Chapter

HIS ROOM

I now stand in the midst of "His Room." Once again I reached and touched all of the "little things" he treasured so dearly each day, yet had no meaning or value to anyone else.

And as I stood there, I wanted to visualize once again times as they once were, only a very short time ago. I yearned once again to hear his voice, his music, and to feel his presence within me.

I glimpsed the many pictures he had placed upon the walls, each relaying to me some small story that had entered his life. I listened for familiar voices of his many friends who were always there in abundance each and every day with him here in this very room, but only now to hear a vibration of silence.

I reflect upon all of the precious moments we had for our "little talks about life" itself and all of the "momentous" problems which were generally solved in a matter of minutes. And how when I used to walk away from this very room, a smile would always project from within me as to how very fortunate I was at that very moment to have him — his innocence was always so overwhelming.

And as I stand here, I wonder how many others at this very moment in time are standing in their "beloved room of memories" as I now am! How many others are holding what I am now cherishing within me?

And how many times each day I would hear his voice call to me from this very room, "Dad, I love you. See you later!!"

Yes, my precious little man, mom and dad will see you later!

Dick Gallagher
TCF, Central Connecticut

THE GRIEF OF SIBLINGS

THE COMPASSIONATE FRIENDS SIBLING CREDO

We are the surviving siblings of The Compassionate Friends. We are brought together by the deaths of our brothers and sisters. Open your hearts to us, but have patience with us. Sometimes we will need the support of our friends. At other times we need our families to be there. Sometimes we must walk alone, taking our memories with us, continuing to become the individuals we want to be. We cannot be our dead brother or sister; however, a special part of them lives on with us.

When our brothers and sisers died, our lives changed. We are living a life very different from what we envisioned, and we feel the responsibility to be strong even when we feel weak. Yet we can go on because we understand better than many others the value of family and the precious gift of life. Our goal is not to be the forgotten mourners that we sometimes are, but to walk together to face our tomorrows as surviving siblings of The Compassionate Friends.

SIBLING GRIEF

I was a sophomore in high school when my little brother, Arthur, was killed. As a sad coincidence, the woman who killed him was the secretary at my school. I can't remember seeing Arthur lying in the street, though I know I did. All I can recall is being horrified and needing to get away from there. I took my younger sister home and never saw Arthur again. It was the dreadful beginning of a very long and painful journey.

The pain of the grief is unavoidable; so is the family disruption. What can be changed, however, is the length of the grieving process. Unfortunately for our family, we were given no help and we stayed a mess for a long time. I would like to share some of my experiences in the hope that it will help you to cope with your brother's or sister's death.

The first thing I can remember is not knowing how to act or what to do. I felt terribly alone and awkward. I didn't know how I was supposed to act at school. Part of me wanted to tell everybody what had happened and part of me didn't want to talk to anyone at all, but I felt people would think I didn't care when I said nothing. It hurt either way. One way I dealt with my grief was by being sarcastic and laughing whenever something painful came up. I laughed outside, but I think my friends knew I was crying inside. Most people don't know how to help us, but hopefully you will have someone you can talk to.

Home becomes a pain-filled place. Our parents, who have been hurt very badly, aren't the parents we knew before. The biggest mistake I made in my grief was trying to "fix" my parents' pain. I wished for and acted in ways that I hoped would change them back to happy, whole people again. I know now that it was not my responsibility to do this. In fact, I couldn't do it. The bad thing was, by trying to make them better, I stuffed a lot of my own sadness, tears, and worries inside. This added even more problems to my grief. I learned we have to take care of ourselves and trust our parents to take care of themselves.

It was years before I was able to cry about my brother. Then I cried for him and for me. I cried for Arthur because he was dead and I missed him. I cried for myself because of all I had missed. I missed feeling happiness in myself and my family, missed feeling safe and secure, missed the attention my parents were no longer able to give me and the years of carefree childhood that were ripped away. These are all losses that we grieve for besides the loss of our brother or sister.

I now realize that my feelings about my brother's death were not the same as my parents'. I used to think I didn't love my brother because I wasn't as sad as long as they were. They hated the holidays, but I wanted the fun they brought. They couldn't be happy. I could, especially after the first terrible set of holidays. Our parents have the right to be sad because that's how they are feeling. We have the right to be happy if that's how we are feeling. Each one of my brothers and sisters had their own feelings. Sometimes we shared feelings, and many times they were different. None of us, however, no matter how bad we felt, came close to having the depth of pain that my parents did. I didn't understand that then as I do now. This is an important thing to know so we don't feel guilty about getting on with our lives.

Another thing I remember is that I used to think about things I did or did not do with my brother before he died. I felt guilty because I didn't play with him the last time he wanted me to, or when I got mad at him and yelled at him for no good reason. I know now that is just a normal part of a brother-sister relationship. I can now realize what I did or didn't do had nothing to do with his death. It is easy to take on guilt so we have to be careful not to.

One last thing that has stayed with me is a fear of dying and of the death of someone else in my family. After Arthur was killed, I suddenly noticed that death was real. A friend from school died, a cousin died, and two of my pets died. Fortunately, there have been many times I expected death and it didn't happen, but the fear is still there. I frequently remind myself of that and it helps. I also try to use the awareness of death's reality to value others in my life right now.

My brother's death definitely changed my life. It brought pain and unhappiness, but it also brought an awareness of other people's pain and the ability to understand and help others. I hope you can take something from my experience and use it in your grief — and maybe you can pass it on someday, too.

Margaret Ann Gerner
TCF, St. Louis, MO

I'M SORRY FOR THE THINGS I DIDN'T DO

It's too late to say "I'm sorry"
For the things I didn't do.
It's too late to say, "Forgive me,
And I'll make it up to you"
For you're gone now, forever.
Oh, if you only knew,
"Kid Brother," just how much
I miss you.

No more teasing, no more pleasing,
No more borrowing the car.
No more promising to be careful,
No more sneaking in the pickle jar.
God in Heaven, please take care
Of that brother of mine.
He was so sweet, so tender, and kind.

Oh, Dear God, when you see him,
Please tell him for me
That I miss him something awful,
Though I have my memories.
And, Dear God, there is something
That I'm asking of you-
Ask Jimmie to please forgive me
For the things I didn't do.

Laura Mae Martin
TCF, Grand Junction, CO

ADOLESCENTS AND GRIEF

Grief over a sibling can intensify and complicate the emotional growth pattern of an adolescent. The adolescent's primary emotional task is to achieve emancipation from childhood ties to parents. The emancipation is gradual, not an amputation. Consequently, there is a swinging back and forth between independent mature behavior and dependency. Sometimes when the adolescent is in pain over the death of a sibling, his grief intensifies his need for dependence, for nuturing by parents. Yet because of his drive toward maturity, he may not let himself acknowledge the need and seems to draw away from parents. This is an age period when peer identification is paramount, as well it should be if the adolescent is to work out good warm relationships with members of his own sex and then with members of the opposite sex. And so it is easily understood that the grieving adolescent often seeks understanding from friends more than from parents.

Although the general pattern is identical - the striving for independence - as we all know, not everyone reacts in exactly the same way. We, as parents, know how devastating is the death of one's child. To the sibling it is devastating, too. He is at an age when he is needing to learn how to handle many new situations that make demands on his capacity to integrate his world. The death of a brother or sister adds a frightening dimension to his ever-increasing load. And so he may react by handling his fright through resorting to familiar patterns - in other words, he may not act his age. Given support, he feels increased inner strength and can abandon his childlike reactions. This swinging back to dependency when needed is a sign of strength rather than weakness.

But what could happen after that? Having needed to be the little child again, he may feel his self-respect was threatened, and to maintain his own self-respect, he must attack a source outside himself. And so he may protest that parents are not letting him grow up. To prove his adequacy, he may resort to unacceptable behavior. At times the adolescent's anxiety over death may be revealed through self-threatening behavior - a way of proving to himself that he is not afraid of death. Another possible explanation may be his deep sense of loss and his not wanting to go on without the brother or sister.

Some parents have talked of the protectiveness of their children. It is almost as though the parent is the child. This illustrates a certain maturity in the adolescent and an expression of his love. This is not to imply that those who do not demonstrate this particular behavior do not love their parents. But when this behavior is typical of them, acknowledgment of its meaning can increase the adolescent's self-esteem. At the same time he needs to feel that he is important to the parents, just as important as the sibling who died.

Adolescents, because of the developmental tasks they need to master, tasks which are complicated by the grief, are in great need of love and attention from parents. They have a tremendous need for acceptance regardless of their behavior. Especially in the early stages, when parents are overcome by grief, it may be difficult to be as emotionally available as they want to be. However, it is so vital to share feelings and to keep lines of communication open and at the same time respect the adolescent's need to show that he is growing up. It isn't easy.

Ruth Eiseman
TCF, Louisville, KY

PLAYING IN THE SHADOWS

We grew up together,
Big sister, little brother.
I took care of you
Until you were old enough to care
  for yourself.
Though you didn't say it,
I knew you loved me.

We played in the sunlight, you and I;
Remember the games of
  Mother-May-I and Hide and Seek?
Sure we had our fights
As all siblings do.
But through it all we never lost
Our love for each other.

Now you're gone.
I'll never see you again
  except in the memories
    of those sunny days.

You will forever be sixteen -
Far too young to die.
You had your whole life to live.
I'll always grieve, but I must go on.
Still, without you,
  I play alone in the shadows.

Cheryl Larson
TCF, Pikes Peak, CO

GRIEF IN THE YOUNG CHILD

As in other areas of development, an understanding of death grows and expands as the child matures. In a study at Children's Hospital in Boston in 1972 among 75 children between the ages of 6 and 15, findings indicated that ideas about death were quite different at various age levels.

It was found that preschool children have very little capacity to deal with something as abstract as death. Most have no concept of the permanence of death but view it primarily as a separation, the dead sibling has gone away. This idea can lead to problems because the child may fantasize that the parent(s) didn't want the sibling anymore, that the sibling was sent away, that the sibling was bad and, therefore, he went away, or that the child was bad and, therefore, lost his sibling. Some preschool children in the study believed there were ways to make the dead come back to life. The implication was that death need not be permanent if someone would only look after the dead person properly. It is important to keep in mind that childhood reasoning may lead to these and other fantasies regarding the permanence of death.

School age children are able to understand the permanence of death, but still can deal with it only in a very concrete way. They understand that the sibling is not coming back but have much more difficulty dealing with the abstractions about death that we may try to offer them. It may be particularly difficult for them to grasp certain religious beliefs. That the sibling has gone to heaven may be of help if the child has an image of what heaven is. It is important to encourage children to share what has been understood of an explanation in order to find out what they have actually grasped of the experience.

There is probably not a child in existence who has not, particularly when having a fight, wished his sibling was dead. When this turns into a reality, it is quite frightening. The extent to which a child retains the associated guilt is directly proportional to the amount of anger the child had toward the sibling. This is particularly difficult when the sibling died after a long illness and the child felt deprived of his parents' time and attention.

Anger is also a normal part of grief. If it continues over a prolonged period, however, it may be wise to help the child channel the energy of anger in a productive way through an outlet such as sports.

If a child is reluctant to remain in a room formerly shared with the child who has died, it may help to make some changes in the room, to redecorate it in some way. However, do this only after consulting with the child. Like adults, children grieve differently and some may want to make changes, while others may want everything left as it was.

Many children are not only capable of talking about death, but seem to want to do so. They appreciate the attention of understanding adults. Silence teaches them that the topic is taboo. We cannot help them cope with their feelings of loss by silence. The best explanations for children, especially for those under the age of 7 or 8, are those which are simple, direct, and draw as much as possible from the child's own experience. In this way, the concrete thinking of the young child will produce the least possible distortion. Adults who undertake to explain death to a young child would be wise to ask the child to repeat to them what he has understood. This would offer the opportunity to correct any gross distortions or misconceptions on the part of the child. It is far better to explore and attempt to respond to the child's ideas than to allow magical thinking or unspoken fears to prey upon a child's imagination.

What about the child who is reluctant to talk about his feelings? Older children, like some adults, cannot discuss their feelings of grief right away, but perhaps months, or even years, later will be ready to talk. Just as with an adult, it is wise not to pressure a child to put his feeling into words. One might be concerned, however, if in addition to not talking about his feelings, the child is having problems with sleeping or eating, is nail biting, stuttering, has regressed in some way (i.e., bedwetting), or is withdrawing from his friends. The best way we as parents can do is to keep an open attitude in the family, conveying the idea that if the child wants to talk, we are always available. If, however, they don't feel comfortable talking to us, the suggestion may be made that they talk to another adult, such as a minister, teacher, or coach who would be a support to the child. One could also offer to arrange for the child to see a professional counselor. Try to convey the notion that it is all right not to talk about it if they do not want to. Keep the avenues of communication open, but do not attempt to force communication.

Children who have a sibling die feel different from their peers. They are "older" in that they have had an experience that most of their friends can't share. The child's fantasy of being totally protected has changed. Mother and father were unable to protect the child who died. This has an impact on the surviving child.

It has an effect on the parents as well. Parents who have a child die are frequently overprotective of the surviving children. Because they fear that something may happen to a surviving child, parents often explode in anger toward a child whom they think has placed himself in jeopardy. This anger can be misinterpreted by the child as a lack of love. A better way to deal with the fear parents quite normally experience may be to share your concern in a calm and reasonable way with your surviving children. In this way, children can be helped to understand that our concern for their well-being and safety arises from our deep love of them.

Excerpted from a presentation
for the Birminghamn, AL chapter of TCF
by Vivian Katzenstein-Friedman, Ph.D.,
Clinical Psychologist at Smolian Clinic and
Asst. Professor of Psychology at The Univ.
of Alabama Medical Ctr., Birmingham, AL

LIKE THE BUTTERFLY

It fluttered there above my head,
Weightless in the soft breeze.
I reached up my hand,
It lit upon my finger.

Waving glistening wings together,
It looked at me for timeless moments.
I smiled, reached deep and
Finding all those cherished memories.

As it flitted off through the sunlit morn,
I knew we had said hello
Once more.

Lezlie Langford
TCF, North Platte, NE

MARK IN MIND

I wanted to tell him I needed him
and to say that I loved him so dearly
but the truck got him first and I nearly
couldn't answer prayer with an "Amen."
Memories tugged at my ailing heart's rim
and nothing was neither said, nor thought clearly.
Sympathies were sent, but they were just merely
a padding of the heart which thought of him.
No one from the outside ever understood
the space that would take years and years to fill
for they did not truly know my brother Mark.
My parents, my sisters, and I would
go on although some things remained standing still.
Thinking of Mark, who to heaven embarked.

Heather Leslie Johnson
TCF, Atlanta, GA

DID YOU KNOW

Did you know:
you need to rip up sheets
to make a kite that flies.
That you cannot build a fort
without a tree with Y's.
That matchbox cars run better
when they are full of paint.
Or, if you hold your breath too long,
you probably will faint.

Did you know:
a baseball bat
makes a terrific gun.
And, yes, an egg can really fry
when left out in the sun.
And cardboard boxes seem to make
the most terrific trains.
And you can swim in puddles
after gentle summer rains.

Did you know:
that baseball cards
clipped upon your bike
will make the awful clicking noise
that parents never like.
A crabtrap can be used to catch
the most exquisite birds
and pig latin
serves to provide
a private world of words.

And Did You Know My Brothers?
They died a few years back.
They taught me all these marvelous things
That sometimes sisters lack.

Kathi Guthrie
TCF, Cape May County, NJ

BY SIBLINGS

When my Sibling Died, I Felt:
- that a part of me died and I was all alone
- very angry at everything
- my childhood had died, too
- angry and sad that my family life as I had known it was over
- terrified that I would lose someone else I loved
- cheated that I didn't have a brother
- angry at how it happened
- alone
- afraid to get close and let anyone in
- terrible
- I wanted to cry
- I felt angry, depressed, confused, drained, worried
- why did it happen to him and not someone else
- I wanted him back

When My Sibling Died, Some Problems I Had Were:
- Most people thought my parents were the only people suffering
- I was afraid to cry in front of my parents because I didn't want to upset them
- People thought I should be over my grief in a week
- I felt guilty when I felt happy about something
- People refused to talk to you about the death of a sibling because they think you will go crazy
- People asking me how my parents are doing and not bothering to ask me how I'm doing
- People saying it was only a brother or sister you lost and you shouldn't feel as bad as your parents
- Parents yelling at you because you don't show any emotion about your sibling's death and that you don't care at all
- People saying they knew exactly how you felt when it had never happened to them
- When things don't go right, I think about my brother, and things just get worse
- People expected me to be back to normal after a short time and didn't understand when I wasn't
- My parents tend to get overprotective of me
- I became very closed. It was hard to talk to people who never felt the way I did.

I Find It Hard To Talk to My Parents About the Loss of My Sibling Because:
- I don't want to upset them
- I hurt more when they hurt
- I hate to see my mother cry
- I would rather grieve by myself and keep it to myself
- I don't get along with my mother that well
- They don't know how I felt
- I think they will start to cry
- I don't find it hard to talk to my parents.

From the young adult group, TCF, Albany/Delmar Chapter, NY

THE SONG

For when the overture begins
A zest of liveliness is shared
Among the musicians and the crowd.
The melody was always wonderful:
Never missing a beat or the tempo.
Like life, she shared her upbeats
And her downbeats
And all the inbetweens.
But her conductor knew
It was her time to go.
He took her out at her peak,
And left all his musicians
A place to fill until their finale
Was over.

That was her song for all to know.
No matter good or bad,
Joyful or sad,
She took it well and she thanked
Her conductor
For her chance to play in his
Almighty orchestra.

Moira Dirr
TCF, Atlanta, GA

THE SURVIVING CHILDREN

Being a parent is never easy. When one's child dies, it is even more difficult being parents to the children who survive. In those first days and weeks, shock may cause us to make decisions (or allow others to make them) that we will later regret. We may wish later that we had included the children more, that we had not permitted ourselves to be isolated from them, that we had explained things differently. Most of us never expect to face this situation, so we have never thought through in advance what the best course would be.

At some point in our grief, we do become more sensitive to these "forgotten grievers" who have lost a brother or sister. They are having struggles of their own.

The first thing to remember is that everything going on with our other children is not caused by the death. They are still, through it all, growing up, going through the various developmental stages that have always concerned parents. Any special problems they had before will not have magically disappeared. Just as we proclaim repeatedly that there is no one way for a parent to grieve, so each child has his own style and timetable for everything, and we cannot control these. We can only try to understand and help when we can. We cannot make it "go away" any more than we can make any of the other harsh realities of life go away.

The very foundation of life has been shaken. The home, so sheltering and safe, has been invaded by forces our surviving children do not understand and parents, who seemed all-powerful and all-wise, may have been reduced to quavering, uncertain robots. Probably for the first time, death - whatever that is - has claimed someone who is not old. Worse, if there has been the usual quota of sibling rivalry and squabbling, the child may be afraid that he has caused the death by being "bad," or by wishing there were no such bothersome person to have to share with or "take a back seat to."

Just as every child is different, every relationship is different. Feelings toward an older brother or sister who was protector, teacher, idol, and those toward a younger one who may have been a sometime responsibility, hanger-on, biggest fan, are not the same. They may have been best friends or rivals who didn't get along very well. Their responses to the death will be as varied as our own.

A child's place in the family system is changed. The second oldest finds himself suddenly the big brother. The buffer between others may be gone. Most difficult of all, a child may have become an "only child." Any child younger than the one who died has to go through the scary years of being the same age. Similar symptoms and situations are so frightening. Brothers and sisters often do look and behave very much alike, and these resemblances can be a source of discomfort or of pride. There may be efforts to exaggerate these, to replace the missing child, to make things the way they used to be.

What can we as parents do to help? Most of all, our children need reassurance and honesty. They need to know they are loved and that the family and the home will continue. They need all the facts they can understand. Part of this honesty requires that they know of your grief. By your actions, you can teach them it is okay to cry (even fathers!), it is okay to admit you are angry at "life" for being this way, that you too are confused about "why." Maintaining a "stiff upper lip" in front of the children only encourages them to suppress their feelings.

Try to be available when they want to talk, but be prepared for the possibility that they may not want to talk with you about their feelings. Many children hold back because they are afraid they might make you cry. You can try explaining that you are not worried about that, but they may still prefer to talk to someone else. They may be ashamed of some common reactions such as feelings of anger, guilt, jealousy, even relief. Perhaps you can help them find someone they can talk to comfortably. They may have already found such a person without you realizing it.

Be honest in the way you remember the child who has died. It is tempting to reminisce about only the good and wonderful qualities, but was this really a saint? Surely not. Recall, and talk about, the not-so-good-and wonderful things too. Be sure you are remembering a real child, for everyone's sake. A saint is hard to live up to. Talking with other parents at a meeting of TCF can give you practical suggestions about things that have worked for other families. You will hear ideas you may not have thought of. Some will have received help from caring professionals and you may decide to consult someone too. When you recognize your family in what others are saying, you may decide that you and your children are really doing pretty well - hurting and healing together - and that it just takes longer than you thought it would.

Ronnie Peterson
TCF, Star Lake, NY

TO BIG A . . .

Silently,
While I slept
And the world went on,
You changed my life,
FOREVER.

Alicia M. Sims
TCF, Albuquerque, NM

THE GRIEF OF GRANDPARENTS

JONATHON TODD

They say you died at birth—
how wrong they are!
For nine months,
wrapped in love's cocoon,
you seemed
already one of us—
How we laughed and dreamed!
When you came that snowy night
and gently closed your eyes
against all cruelty,
your tiny hands forged
tighter family ties— your special warmth,
a blessed radiance
that hallows all our lives.

Marion H. Youngquist
Grandmother
TCF, Ocean County Chapter, NJ

EULOGY FOR A LOST BABY

A grandfather remembers Jamie, who was born on St. Valentine's Day and died in his crib 46 days later.

I had intended to write a humorous piece about first grandfatherhood. My son, David, and his wife, Nancy, had just produced a healthy baby boy, and suddenly I was embarked on a rite of passage. I imagined myself a kindly sage, baiting a hook for a freckle-faced tyke—but I didn't know anything about fishing. Perhaps he could watch me whittle a stick—but I couldn't whittle either. I'd go on in this vein, striking just the right self-deprecating tone, peppering my conceits with sly satire. Finally, I'd conclude that these Norman Rockwell images were out of character. I'd be myself, take my grandson to the zoo, buy him Cracker Jacks. I'd bring him to the office, where he'd make paper-clip chains and send silly messages through the pneumatic tubes. I'd build him a dark room and teach him to make pictures.

My funny piece would also tease the new grandmothers, who were seriously engaged in a ritual of their own, trying to find suitable names for themselves—Nana, Nanny, Mimi, Mumu, Baba, Mama, anothing but Grandma—but, by gosh, I'd stick to good old Gramps or Grandpa. No big deal. Twenty years from now my grandson would read this piece, and maybe he'd say, "Good old Gramps, rest his soul. He didn't know anything about fishing or whittling, but we sure had some fine times."

I was still ruminating when the news came. This little baby was gone, dead at 46 days of age. Sudden Infant Death Syndrome — SIDS — crib death. He lay asleep one moment, stopped breathing the next. Born on St. Valentine's Day, died April Fool's Day, buried on Good Friday. A precious promise wiped out by a wanton prank.

From TCF Newsletter, Champaign-Urbana, IL

TO BEREAVED GRANDPARENTS

I am powerlessness. I am helplessness,. I am frustration.

I sit here with her and cry with her. She cries for her daughter and I cry for mine. I can't help her. I can't reach inside and take her broken heart. I must watch her suffer day after day and see her desolate.

I listen to her tell me over and over how she misses Emily, how she wants her back. I can't bring Emily back for her. I can't even buy her an even better Emily than she had, like I could buy her an even better toy when she was a child.

I can't kiss the hurt and make it go away. I can't even kiss a small part of it away. There's no bandaid large enough to cover her bleeding heart.

There was a time I could listen to her talk about a fickle boyfriend and tell her it would be okay, and know in my heart that in two weeks she wouldn't even think of him. Can I tell her it'll be okay in two years when I know it will never be okay, that she will carry this pain of "what might have been" in her deepest heart for the rest of her life?

I see this young woman, my child, who was once carefree and fun-loving and bubbling with life, slumped in a chair with her eyes full of agony. Where is my power now? Where is my mother's bag of tricks that will make it all better?

Why can't I join in the aloneness of her grief? As tight as my arms wrap around her, I can't reach that aloneness.

Where are the magic words that will give her comfort? What chapter in Dr. Spock tells me how to do this? He has told me everything else I've needed to know. Where are the answers? I should have them. I'm her mother.

What can I give her to make her better? A cold wet wash cloth will ease that swelling of her crying eyes, but it won't stop the reason for her tears. What treat will bring joy back to her? What prize will bring that "happy child" smile back again?

I know that someday she'll find happiness again, that her life will have meaning again. I can hold out hope for her someday, but what about now? this hour? this day?

I can give her my love and prayers and my care and my concern. I could give her my life. But even that won't help.

Margaret Gerner
TCF, St. Louis, MO

TO MY GRANDDAUGHTER

Thanks to one of God's Special Nurses, Marie, I got to see you, hold you, and touch you.

The minute she placed you in my arms, I felt an overwhelming feeling of love.

And I knew somehow, someway, you felt it too.

As I sat there looking at your beautiful little face and tiny body, I hoped and prayed you would open your eyes and let out a cry.

But none ever came.

I knew that God had made you one of his little angels in Heaven.

As I handed you back to Marie, I kissed you on the cheek and wept.

But I thank God with all my heart and soul, and his special nurse, for the short time we had together. Someday we will meet again in Heaven.

I LOVE YOU NICHOEL!!

Love,
Grandma

Joyce Johnson
TCF, North Shore/Boston, MA

CHAPTER V

THERE IS NO GOOD AGE OR WAY TO LOSE A CHILD

Look at yourself
in the mirror.
Say to yourself
"It is hard
to lose a child."
Say to yourself
"It is reasonable
to hurt."
Say to yourself
"Healing takes
time."
BE GOOD TO YOURSELF.

Sascha

SUDDEN OR ACCIDENTAL DEATH

AN ELEGY TO DAN

Pounding on the door late in the night,
a policeman brings us the message.
The car moves maddeningly slow.
Will we ever get there?

Nervous talking, leaden silence.
The parking lot looms in the darkness,
helicopter blades gleaming in the moonlight.
The guard runs to meet us.

A kind nurse tries to squelch our hope.
She calmly gestures back and forth,
her words, "no chance," hanging in the air.
The wait seems long.

We sit huddled in that cold corridor,
refusing to understand, each pretending.
Bedpans rattle, patients murmur and moan.
Word comes, sister cries, pastor prays.

I demand to see my son, waiting at the
emergency door, eyes just able to see
over the small square panes.
Finally they roll him out.

Even then my heart swells with pride.
I place my hand on his beardless cheek,
already turning cold.

"Oh, Dan," I say. A nurse coughs, holding
the sheet to her face; another holds out
his gold neck chain.
Sister's tears fall on his forehead.

We leave. No one speaks.
The hospital looks black against a gray
Atlanta sky.
There's activity in the street,
People are going to work.

My God, people are going to work!

Elnora McConnell Borden
TCF, Atlanta, GA

SUDDEN ACCIDENTAL DEATH

This will touch on a few of the real problems we encounter in traumatic grief experienced from the sudden accidental death of a child: shock, guilt, unfinished business, lack of closure, negative attitudes or obstacles to recovery, and anger.

I don't pretend to have any concrete answers, but hopefully a few insights on how to cope with grief. We all grieve differently. What works for one may not work for another.

We don't want to make judgments on which kind of grief is more difficult, but sudden death is recognized as one of the most difficult to recover from because of the tremendous shock involved. It will be longer, lonelier, and more hazardous to your lasting emotional stability than if you had been able to anticipate the loss and to communicate with your child before death.

One of the large differences between sudden accidental death and death by long-term illness or anticipatory death, is the shock involved. It is the primary factor. This shock affects the body as major surgery would. Shock is marked by a lowering of blood pressure, coldness of skin, rapid heartbeat and an acute sense of terror. Therefore, we may experience immediate physical problems upon learning of the death of our child. The physical problems we encounter include excessive tiredness, headaches, stomach problems, and strange heart activity. These may come at any time in our bereavement and often come and go.

Emotional or psychological shock is indeed of even larger significance. It is of unfathomable proportions. Initially there is alarm because in an instant our whole lives are changed; there is disbelief; the overwhelming reality is more than we can comprehend. We think there must be a mistake. Often we experience a numbness. Later we go through this feeling of numbness again, and it may last for weeks or months.

When the numbness wears off, we go into our intense grief experience. There are tears, depression. We relive the events surrounding the death over and over. Usually by this time the family and friends have gone back to their own lives, and we are alone with this awful burden of grief. At this time the highly emotional experience may cause us to think we are mentally unstable, that we are losing our minds. Just remember that you are not alone, that the others of us who have had our children die in this manner have felt the same things, but don't hesitate to seek professional help if you feel you need it or if you appear to be "stuck" in any of the stages.

With sudden death there is usually a feeling of guilt. It may be self-imposed or real. We remember punishments that were unresolved, arguments that were not reconciled, and there is always the question of "Could I have prevented it?" We ask ourselves the question "WHY" over and over. I know now that this question is often unanswerable, but we all ask anyway.

In sudden death we have no chance for closure; no chance to say goodbye. This adds to the burden as we think of what we could have or should have done. We are hindered in accepting our child's death by negative attitudes that arise from our questions and our need to place blame. We have been hurt beyond our wildest dreams and must allow ourselves to express whatever emotions we may feel. It may not be pleasant for those around us, but it is necessary. We must work through our emotions; get them out. There are many forms of denial; learn to recognize them and work through them. People release their emotions in different ways. Crying is helpful and necessary. Talking is of utmost importance. This is one of the primary functions of The Compassionate Friends. We'll listen to one another where our friends are likely to hand us a drink or a tranquilizer as they grow weary of listening to us. We need to talk for months and sometimes years about our experience. Many of our feelings may frighten us, but know that they are normal, natural, and to be expected. Even thoughts that we are losing our minds are normal. We've all felt that way. Just remember we are NOT losing our minds; it only feels that way.

The circumstances of sudden death cause loneliness. Few people can identify with us because our circumstances are practically unique. This uniqueness isolates us.

Another of our severe problems is often anger, which might be better described as rage. It can be anger focused on individuals who were responsible for the death of our child, at medical personnel who we feel did not do the right things to save our child, at God for letting this happen to our child, anger at people around us whose lives are happy and whose children are healthy. We may even feel anger at our child for dying and leaving us with such a burden of grief. Anger is normal but, if denied and repressed, can be turned inward and become expressed as depression. Depression can lead to thoughts of suicide. Get help if it lasts too long.

Anger gives us tremendous energy and that energy can be used. It can be focused on healthy outlets. For instance: take up a cause, work for stricter law enforcement against drunk drivers or gun con-

trol issues. Use that energy positively; it will give a sense of accomplishment and renewed self-esteem. Bereaved parents are in grave danger of drug and alcohol abuse, for these are tools that sometimes give temporary relief. Drugs and alcohol are merely means of putting off the grief process. Grief work will have to be done eventually and our literature tells us it is worse when put off or delayed.

With the death of a child we as parents experience the ultimate failure - we are supposed to be invincible where our children are concerned and now we have failed to keep our child alive! Suddenly our belief system is shattered. The suddenness of the death has robbed us of our confidence in ourselves. We have low self-esteem. We suffer from lack of motivation due to our severe fatigue. We have nothing left to believe in, not even God, for some. We are totally insecure. We are placed in the position of continuing to deteriorate or to begin to rebuild our lives by rebuilding our beliefs, our self-confidence and our self-esteem. The choice is ours. Choose to live. Our children would want us to not only just live, but to continue to grow and love.

Fay Harden
TCF, Tuscaloosa, AL

LONG-TERM ILLNESS

MY STRUGGLE WITH GRIEF

The pain and sorrow, the feelings of emptiness and loneliness, and the loss of purpose and hope that swept over me when our 13-year-old son, John, died may be feelings that overwhelmed you, too, when your child died.

Ours had been an Il-month battle with an unconquerable foe. Our funloving, athletic, curious and clever son was diagnosed as having a rare type of cancer, Burkitts lymphoma. We were devastated at the diagnosis, but were convinced that a cure was possible. Our John had always been so healthy, always determined and very competitive. He was sure that he could beat this disease and with determination, love, courage, medicine and prayer, I, too, thought he could. He fought a valiant fight. He took all the treatment with courage. He was able to maintain his sense of humor and interest in life. John went from an active competitor in sports to a collector of miniatures, coins, comic books, and stamps. He rarely complained and accepted his disappointments with dignity. He shared his innermost thoughts and aspirations, and as a family we all came to admire his courage and determination. When he died, we were devastated.

There are two things that I think make losing a child as a result of a prolonged illness particularly traumatic and difficult. The first is the closeness that develops between the child and his family, particularly his mother or the person caring for him most as the child becomes more dependent for support, understanding and physical care. That closeness developed to such an extent during his illness that the person I came to know best and care about most was that struggling child.

From my own experience and from others I have talked to who have had similar experiences, I am convinced that having a child who has a life-threatening disease is as close to having that disease and suffering through the treatment as is possible without actually having it. I used to dream that I was having radiation and chemotherapy during John's treatment. Perhaps this results from a real desire on the part of the parent to take the child's place since there seems to be little else they can do. So the loss leaves such an empty place, one that cannot be filled, and for me there was a real desire to go to be with that child.

Perhaps just as devastating is the unbelievable frustration of losing the battle. John referred to his chemotherapy protocol as his "sentence in a prison camp," and he believed that he would live through it and come out a better person as others had before him. We always thought that we would win the battle for his life; our family would win; our John would win. We gave our every effort and self-

sacrifice to that end. Most of all, John gave his every effort. He was determined, persistent and courageous. He maintained his sense of humor, his thoughtfulness for others and his absolute faith in his doctors and his family and in his God. And still he did not live. The initial shock was overwhelming. It is a frustration that I still have to deal with. How could it be that with all this going for him and with the knowledge that children do survive cancer, our beloved John should die. In spite of the fact that I have made many efforts to deal with this dilemma, I still have not come up with a satisfactory answer.

John was faced with an unalterable situation. He was stricken with a terminal illness, the cause of which will not be determined. He lived his life with courage, faith, hope and love. We supported him with all the love and understanding that we could. He had the finest medical care available. Still he died. There was and is no way to change these facts. I miss him every day and expect that I always will. No one can ever take away the empty feeling I live with because John died, nor the wish I have that he were still here growing up like his friends and enjoying life to the fullest, as he always did.

The situation I faced after John's death was frightening. The days kept coming and I had to continue my life without one of the very persons that gave it meaning and joy. After much sorrow and contemplation and with the support and love of family and friends, including The Compassionate Friends, I came to the decision that I was not going to merely exist and live through the days, but that I was going to try to use my gift of life to the utmost as John had used his. Other parents like me have lost children and there are some who continue to find joy, hope and meaning in life, but not without effort.

There is joy in my life now. There is laughter in our home and good times. There is hope for the future now. We have sought positive ways to remember John. Members of our family continue to give books to a memorial shelf of books in the library of the elementary school John attended. This memorial was started by friends of John who knew of his love of history and social studies. Members of our family periodically give blood to the Red Cross, hoping to help others who may need that gift in their struggle for life. A scholarship has been established at Georgia Tech in John's name with preference being given to students who have overcome a similar disease. Our other two children continue to bring me joy and give meaning to my life. We have a foster daughter now who adds her frustrations and joys in life to our family.

Life will never be the same. I will always be disappointed that John did not have a longer life, but I will always be proud of him and love him. I continue to search for ways to bring love, hope and meaning to my life as I try to make use of my one gift of life.

Dorothy Schafer
TCF, Atlanta, GA

SPECIAL CHILDREN

Our God must have a special love for certain children here
Who from their births or early times know illness, pain and tears,
And who, too soon, their lives completed, then are taken back.
Such children often show an insight other people lack.

They seem to have a spirit strong in which real courage thrives.
And in a very special way they touch our adult lives.
For even though they don't let on, their fate they surely know,
And facing death, they go on smiling, cheer their parents so.

We read of Alex, hear of others — Teresa, Angie, Brandt -
And how, in spite of illness grave, their time is well spent.
So, though God's not the cause of illness which we speak of here,
He surely gives a special spirit to these children dear.

Robert F. Gloor
TCF, Tuscaloosa, AL

NO GUARANTEE

The prognosis is made and
the tears are shed.
The reality begins and
the battle is everlasting.
They do what they can and
offer sympathy and support.
The family ties are simultaneously
strengthened and weakened,
never smooth, always tense.
Laughter comes seldom, but
most always remembered.
Portraits are treasured,
carefully protected and cherished.
Hospitalizations and appointments
are met with, but never easy.
The voice that speaks, but never heard,
is saying the same old verse -

Life isn't simple,
when there's no guarantee.

Maria C. Angelina
before she died of cystic
fibrosis. Daughter of
Diane McCarthy
TCF, Western Adirondack Chapter

MURDERED CHILDREN

ON DEALING WITH A VIOLENT DEATH

The following thoughts on coping are offered by Father Ken Czillinger of Cincinnati, Ohio, who for many years has worked with the dying and grieving and who is responsible for forming many support groups in his area.

1. *Generally it takes 18-24 months just to stabilize after the death of a family member. It can take much longer when the death was a violent one. Recognize the length of the mourning process. Beware of developing unrealistic expectations of yourself.*
2. *Your worst times usually are not at the moment of the tragedy. Then you're in a state of shock or numbness. Often you slide "into the pits" four to seven months after the event. Strangely, when you're in the pits, tempted to despair, this may be the time when most expect you to be over your loss.*
3. *When people ask you how you're doing, don't always say, "Fine." Let some people know how terrible you feel.*
4. *Talking with a true friend or with others who've been there and survived can be very helpful. Those who've been there speak your language. Only they can really say, "I know; I understand." You are not alone.*
5. *Often depression is a cover for anger. Learn to uncork your bottle and find appropriate ways to release your bottled-up anger. What you're going through seems so unfair and unjust.*
6. *Take time to lament, to experience being a victim. It may be necessary to spend some time feeling sorry for yourself. "Pity parties" sometimes are necessary and can be therapeutic.*
7. *It's all right to cry, to question, to be weak. Beware of allowing yourself to be "put on a pedestal"by others who tell you what an inspiration you are because of your strength and your ability to cope so well. If they only knew!*
8. *Remember you may be a rookie at the experience you're going through. This is probably the first violent death you've coped with. You're new at this, and you don't know what to do or how to act. You need help.*
9. *Reach out and try to help others in some small ways at least. This little step forward may help prevent you from dwelling on yourself.*
10. *Many times of crisis ultimately can become times of opportunity. Mysteriously your faith in yourself, in others, in God can be deepened through crisis. Seek out persons who can serve as symbols of hope to you.*

THE MURDER OF MY SON, SAM

My son had been dead not quite thirteen months when I finally found what I had been searching for for months - one inch of newsprint telling of the existence of a support group in Atlanta for bereaved parents - The Compassionate Friends. I needed desperately to talk to someone who had also suffered the loss of a child.

My second son, Sam, age 2l, had been murdered on the street in downtown Atlanta. He made the last mistake he will ever make on that December night: he resisted a robbery. Up until then I only thought I had problems. I had lost my father, my marriage of twenty years, had survived cancer and the heartbreak of having one of my sons rebel against the very things I had instilled in him. But all of this was minor compared to the shock and pain of Sam's death. When someone came to tell me of his murder, I felt as though I had been split down the middle with a chain saw without anesthesia.

I had been trying to work through all my emotions for over a year, but the horror and heartache of having him die so needlessly and senselessly, of having him robbed of the dignity of the choice of life - the right to live, my feelings about his murderers, whoever they were, my anger at his friend who ran and deserted him at the time of the robbery, the seeming lack of interest of the homicide department, the unwanted attention of the media, the morgue, the autopsy, the burial, my anger at the mayor for his refusal of the courtesy of an answer to my letters, was all too much. And, all the while I felt I was losing my mind because my "normal" friends, those who had not outlived a child, were telling me I should be "all over it" by now, and I believed them. I needed to know I was sane.

Attending The Compassionate Friends meetings helped me to know that my feelings, whatever they were, were normal for me. I learned it was okay to be both angry at my son for his stupidity and carelessness in resisting a robbery and also proud of him for standing up for a principle that said what was his, was his. The compassionate people who attend these meetings helped me save my second marriage because I didn't understand my husband's grief. They helped me to better understand my surviving children's problems, as well as to learn there are no good ways to lose a child. They helped me to learn to express my anger at God for what I felt were His failings, and then to forgive Him and find peace, understanding and love from my God again.

I loved my son more than myself. We had loved and fought for half of my lifetime. He was a big giver and a big taker and was the "life" of our family. He had a sense of self-worth, knowing who he was and where he was going. He had a lot to give. I lost a large part of my future when he died, as well as my pride, my joy, and happiness. I was consumed for a long time with what I had lost.

Today, I am no longer angry at Sam. I have given him the right to make his own choices with his life. I remember the good and bad of him, for he had both. My son's life had a purpose, and with the help of TCF, the many hours on the phone and in the meetings, his death has had a purpose for today I am a stronger, better person for having experienced Sam's life and his death. I still don't know who murdered him, but I have been able to put that aside, recognizing I may never know and this is something I can do nothing about. I refuse to let it consume me for the rest of my life. I am now a more complete person, ready to move forward.

If you are struggling with the aftermath of a murder, I hope you hear my message that it will be better. It takes time, but most worthwhile things do.

Jayne Collins
TCF, Atlanta, Ga.

SORTING OUT

Almost five years.
At first details of her murder
roiled inside my skull
like a storm-driven surf
tossing without lull.
And always the tears.

Now mellow memories are doled
unexpectedly from time to time
as lilac scent teased
by a whimsical spring breeze
nourishing the soul.

Father's Day
and a daughter who will never really die.
The fond flicker of a smile in the eye
Reflective
Proud
Loving.

Neil Hanlon
TCF, Stamford, CT

SHARDS OF GRIEF LINGER AFTER MURDER

On a dreary night in December, a knock came at our door with news that would forever alter our lives. The news was that Anne, our daughter, had been kidnapped and brutally murdered by persons or a person unknown. The shock, disbelief, anquish and anxieties over the next several months, a small piece of the grieving process, were extraordinary, and I have often wondered how we survived.

There was the extreme rage at the person who was responsible for taking Anne's life for no reason except for the pure pleasure of destroying good. But we survived.

There was the awful anger against the legal system for being so callous and insensitive to the needs of the family and friends. The wounds from Anne's death were already deep and unhealing, but listening to and reading about the insinuations and innuendos by the lawyers made the wounds grow deeper and deeper. The impression was given the family must endure punishment for allowing our daughter to be in the wrong place. This caused a feeling of guilt, but we survived.

There was the fear that Anne would become just another statistic, and the person responsible would go unpunished. Now the fear exists that the person will be released from prison to repeat his acts of violence. I am afraid that fears are addictive and one replaces another. Perhaps the worst fear is, when your faith in God is at its lowest ebb, that you will never be able to respond to normal stimuli again and regain that faith. All the fears are real, but so far we have survived. These, I suppose, are normal reactions as the result of a violent act. I believe these anxieties delay a normal (so called) grieving period until after the culprit has been found, tried, and sentenced. After these three things happened, I do know a terrible burden was lifted from our shoulders, and we could restart living our lives. Somehow we survived.

How did we survive? After much reflecting, I firmly believe we survived by recalling the positive aspects of Anne's life and character. Each individual is endowed with certain instruments and we hear the music of their lives long after they are gone. Anne's instrument of love of life was a blessing, and we can still hear the melodies of her song in the night. These melodies cannot be taken away, and they are more valuable than diamonds to us.

Anne's instrument of hope for a future in which to achieve her goals and have some effect on society was the backbone of her dreams. The songs of hope in work, in life, and the goodness of heart cannot be destroyed by evil or circumstances. Today is gone, but we still hear the songs of hope for tomorrow. These songs of hope, heard in the night, sustain us.

Anne's instrument of faith that she would lead a productive life and achieve both her spiritual and material goals was music in her heart. The faith she had in herself, her family, and her friends transmits to us, urging us to proceed with our lives. The music of her faith is still a beacon in the night.

We will not believe Anne's dreams have ended, but will believe they will find their place in the world to come. The music that was set in motion by her love, hope, and faith will move, everlasting, in sweet memories forever. The wounds from the loss of a loved one cannot be healed by words or deeds. These terrible burdens are borne by each of us in our own way and, hopefully, we survive.

Bill Boggs
TCF, Augusta, GA

AFTER A SUICIDE

SUICIDE

S is for the Smiles, Sweetness and Speciality you brought
S is for the Sadness, Sorrow, Shame and Stigma you left;

U is for the Understanding that eludes me;

I is for the Inadequancy and Insecurity you must have felt
I is for the Imprudence and Injustice of your act;

C is for the Crying I cannot stop;

I is for the Impulsive and Impatient Irish girl you were
I is for the Incredible Incompetency I feel;

D if for Dead, there is no turning back;

E is for the Eyes donated to Enlighten another's life
E is for the Eighteen years you lived, and love was not Enough!

Priscilla J. Norton
TCF, Greater Providence, RI

THE ANSWER IS BECAUSE

Early in the evening
Reluctant to the dawn
Scot would choose to die
Before the early morn
He chose the final method
The one that hurts the worst
He chose to die the loss —
The loss of his self worth.
I miss him something terrible
I wish he knew I cared
I wish he knew I loved him
And really would have shared.
I hope he's happy now
I hope he's found his peace
I hope he's found the things he
wants
The things he really needs.

Stacey Blumenthal
in memory of her brother
TCF, St. Louis, MO

A GIFT FROM MITCH

Trying to talk about Mitch's suicide, even ten years later, still brings many thoughts to mind regarding all of my feelings...then and now. The feelings are so personal, so private, so utterly my own that the thoughts of sharing them with another is still difficult today.

Yet, in the midst of the growing awareness of suicide and at the efforts being made today to slow the occurrence, my hope is that we can provide insights into the feelings we have had, are having, and will continue to experience.

Surely nothing in my life has taken so much out of me and at the same time given me so much hope for others. Hardly a day passes without someone coming to my office to talk about their interest in sales, and beginning to talk about the tragedy that has taken place in their immediate family or with loved ones. My hope is that through the opportunity of talking about our loss, others may find that they too can proceed to make the journey through the pain and anguish that can be mastered.

I admit that in the aftermath of Mitch's death there were so many questions that it is hard to bring them to the conscious level. One of many was "Whose fault is it?" and an anger that could not be easily put aside. There is the dichotomy I faced in trying to bring to terms the different feelings that racked my body and mind. Who could possibly know what I was feeling? No man, no woman, no priest, no counselor . . . no one knew.

I began to ask myself the questions of how I would deal with my friends, co-workers, the business contacts. Who would stand ahead of me and let them know that I had suffered and should be handled with care? I thought everyone in the world knew Mitch shot himself and that this father of his was about to enter a room, call on the telephone, or write a letter.

To my surprise, a lot of people did not know, but those who did went out of their way to give me the support of love and comfort. My faith would tell me that I should expect help from our church, but I had no concept of the strength, love and support that waited for me. Sure I knew the church; after all, we had been with the church from almost the very beginning as a mission. But the strength that awaited us there was more and bigger and wider and . . .

Probably nothing stands out in my mind more than the different people who expressed their love and support. This came from the church and from others around us. It seemed that as soon as I could permit myself to express, to expose, I received the reinforcement to proceed.

Time became the major factor, slowly rebuilding the strengths that I knew I had, to overcome the agony. I found that time moved impossibly slow. When would I feel better, when would it be over? The truth is that it is never over, but then it is not supposed to be over. The truth is that will never be, but my growth and gaining strength will make it acceptable.

Years have passed since I went back to Mitch's room to find him dying by his own hands. That image is still with me today, and yet I find that I can look at the image and be at peace with myself. I know I did not plan, nor want, nor envision, that my son could or would take his life. But it is a fact, and I can live with it today, knowing that I have made it this far.

It was a gift Mitch has given us - a new knowledge of strength. Mitch has given us a new understanding of loving, caring, and the warmth of the friendship of others. Mitch has renewed our faith in God and the world. This was a friendship that I had taken for granted. No more! Time is precious. Life is precious. You are precious. Each day is a new revelation of this gift, a gift from Mitch.

Jack Bolton
TCF, North Atlanta Chapter

ON A ROSEBUSH FULL OF BLOOMS

On a rosebush full of blooms, there is occasionally one rose more fragile than the rest. Nobody knows why. The rose receives the same amounts of rain and sun as its neighboring blooms; it receives the same amounts of water and food from the earth, of clipping and tending and gentle encouragement from the gardener. Its time on earth is neither more nor less significant than that of the other blooms alongside. Its stresses are neither greater nor fewer. Its promises of development are just as rich. In other words, it has all the necessary components to become what it is intended to be: a beautiful flower, fully open, spreading its petals and fragrance and color for the world to see.

But for some inexplicable reason, once in awhile a single rose doesn't reach maturity. It's not the gardener's fault. It's not the fault of the rose. For some roses, even the touch of the gentle spring rains leaves bruises on the petals. The sun's rays—so soft and warm to some flowers—feel searing to others. Some roses thrive while fragile ones feel buffeted by inner and outer ghostwinds.

So it is that sometimes, despite the best growing conditions, the best efforts of the gardener, and the best possibilities and predictions for a glorious blooming season, a particularly fragile rose will share its glow for awhile, then fade and die. And the gardener and the rosebush and the earth and all around grieve.

We are never ready for a loss, not for the loss of a promising rosebud, nor for the loss of a friend or relative whose life appears ready to unfold with brilliant color and fulfillment. In the midst of our grieving, we can remember and celebrate the glimpses of color and fragrance and growth that were shared. We can love the fragile rose and the fragile soul for the valiant battles won and the blooming that was done. And as our own petals unfold, we can remember the softness and beauty of those who touched us along the way.

Earnestine Clark
TCF, Oklahoma City, OK

INFANT DEATH

SOMETIMES LATE AT NIGHT

Sometimes late at night
When I'm alone,
Sometimes in the middle of the day
When I'm with friends,

I want to hold you
And feel the touch of your tiny hands.
I long to see a sparkle in your little eyes,
Just to see a smile on your face.
I wish I could hear a cry from my baby boy.

I think after a year
I should be over the pain
Of not having you near.
Then I realize I never will be.

Lynn Yekalis
TCF, Atlanta, GA

PARENTS OF INFANTS - ON LOSING A BABY

Unlike parents who have had an older child die, our memories are few and for some parents even non-existent. Those of us who have had a baby die have found it common for some people not to recognize the loss as being as tragic as the death of an older child. Maybe it is just as tragic, maybe it isn't. For most parents who have lost a baby, the tragedy is felt as intensely as can be. For many parents who lose a baby, there is nothing else with which to compare their loss. It is just like we who have lost a child (at no matter what age) feel that no one can understand the way we feel unless they too have had a child die. Those of us who have not had an older child die have nothing else to compare the death of our baby with, just as those who have had an older child cannot completely understand our feelings upon the death of a baby

The death of an infant is oftentimes considered "unfortunate," but so many feel that it can be remedied with the birth of another child. Some people find it difficult to understand the love, hope, and the future that has been lost with the death of a "much looked forward to" baby.

In my own situation, I have found that the words of consolation most often given to me are things like "You're young; you can have other babies," "It's better you were never able to hold her and love her," or, "It's over with, forget it, put it all behind you." The truth of the matter, for me at least, was yes, I could have more babies, but it did not matter how many children I could have in the future, I still had lost Jessica. She was the baby daughter I had wanted and tried to have for eight years. Upon her death, all my hopes and dreams and my happiness, I felt, were gone. The daughter I had looked so forward to holding and loving and spending time with was gone. Yes, since her death I have been blessed with the birth of two children, a son and another daughter. I give thanks daily for their health and loving presence. But just as another child could never take their place, nor have they replaced Jessica.

Was it really better that I never got to hold her? I think not. If only I had been able to hold that blessed little angel in my arms, if only for one short moment, I would be better able to cope with my loss. If I had been able to see her (even though she was already dead), I would have had a memory to hold on to the rest of my life. Learn to love her? I already loved her. Any mother who carries a child knows love for that child even though it is still unborn. I loved her. I knew her. I knew that she would become quiet and still when I spoke softly to her. I knew she would react with somewhat violent kicking when surrounded by loud noises. I knew her while she was yet inside me. She was real. I loved her.

I cannot ever forget her. I never want to. I still wonder what she would have grown to be like, what she would have grown to look like. Would she have been fair and active like my son, Justin, or would she have been dark and quietly composed like Ashlee? I think about these things even after four years. I expect to think about them for the rest of my life. I wonder what it would have been like around her with three children close in age, playing together. I wonder what it would have been like with three children to love, I wonder... I guess for a parent of a baby who dies, the wonderings are the worst. We just do not know. We have no memories to cherish.

I am not trying to make a comparison with the death of a child who lived to be older. I cannot compare things which I do not know about. I just know that a parent who has a baby die feels grief and loss and pain and hurt. To grieve is to grieve, to feel pain and loss is to feel the pain and loss, to miss a child is to miss a child. Of course there are, as in everything various degrees of feeling, and to each parent his or her child was special; and the feelings still go deep and the loss is still felt at no matter what age a child dies.

Deby Amos
TCF, Anniston, AL

MEMORIAL ON A BRIEF LIFE

For eight months he grew inside me,
His heart beat,
His legs kicked,
His arms moved.
Then one day it stopped.

Hardly a human lifespan
Yet an eon of remembered fact:
Of anticipation,
Of what our baby would be like,
Of a crib filled with love and happiness,
Of a tiny baby we would carefully watch grow.

For eight months he grew inside me
Long enough to have memory forever remind me
That I never saw him
Never held him,
Never felt his softness,
Never counted his toes,
Never knew the color of his eyes.

Long enough to tell me and retell me of the
Death-paled hands not quite covered by the gown
he never got to wear home,
Of all the stuffed animals he never got to use,
Of a small casket,
The smell of moist earth,
And tears.

In my hand I hold an obituary,
A statistical report,
A map to the cemetery lot where he was buried,
A picture of his casket . . .
Souvenirs . . .
We are all sorry,
We know how you feel, they say.
Thanks,
But you can't know,
For I don't feel,
Not yet.

It all went so fast - love - anticipation
Where has it all gone?

Memories . . .

Mary Eggen
TCF, Central Coast Chapter, CA

INTENSIVE CARE NURSERY

I didn't forget to run my fingers along
her pug nose and talk to her in my lingo
and call her Arin's nickname by mistake
and give her Elle's message, which was
Come home, little sister.

I didn't forget to take pictures of her
and note the color of her eyes.

I didn't forget to cry in front of her
and beg her to get better.

But I forgot to sing her a lullabye,

And I forgot to ask if it was all right
to kiss her, and if it could be ar-
ranged so I could hold her, and how
much time we had left.

And I forgot to take a close look at
her thumbs, to see if they're fat
and funny like mine.

And I forgot - Oh, God, I forgot
to explain to her that it was my
body that betrayed her, not me.

Marion Cohen
TCF, Philadelphia, PA

OLIVIA'S CANDLE

My husband and I lost our baby, Olivia, during pregnancy, and having no funeral or other traditional means of finding a place for our feelings of loss and love for this cherished person, a person many believed never lived at all, we settled on burning a candle for 24 hours every time the death date passes. Beside the candle is this poem.

To our beloved Olivia, whose
life-light burned so briefly
You are forever a part of us
as we remember and relive
The joy with which we discovered
you and
The sadness with which we accepted
your departure.
The light and the love you lit
in us burns on . . .

Patti Williams
TCF, Northeast Georgia Chapter

SOMETIMES

Sometimes love is for a moment
Sometimes love is for a lifetime,
Sometimes a moment is a lifetime.

Pamela S. Adams
TCF, Winnipeg, Canada

SINCE DOUGLAS DIED

A week has passed,
And I'm so alone
Though I couldn't tell you why.
I guess it's just the emptiness
I've felt since Douglas died.

They say it's SIDS,
and that doesn't say much
of why he had to leave.
Now it's up to us to say
we'll make it, though we'll grieve.

The kids just don't know what
it means that their little baby died.
They only sense that something's
wrong when they see mommy and daddy cry.

Christy knows Doug won't be back
because heaven's just too far,
And Cathy says, let's go get him in
the family car.

Doozer's just flat out confused, and
T. J. don't know why there's just
four of them to go on Disney's rides.

As time goes by, the hurt will heal,
But I'm sure there'll be a scar,
for my heart is giving love for five,
but four are all there are.

Tim Smith
TCF, Sarasota, FL

OLDER PARENTS' GRIEF

THE BIRTHDAY

She had not noticed me as she entered the cemetery as I sat quietly beside my son's grave. For a while, lost in my own thoughts of my son's 28th birthday, I forgot about her. Then the sound of her tear-filled, croaky, off-key singing caught my attention. She sat by her son's grave, all alone, and sang "Happy Birthday." Her eyes seemed to strain to see through the stone as she sang with tears in her voice - HAPPY BIRTHDAY TO YOU. In a flash my mind carried me back to other birthdays of my own son. I saw a chocolate-cake-smeared one-year-old face, a blond-haired baby face, a crewcut little boy face, a carefully groomed and scrubbed adolescent face, a long-haired-holey-blue jeaned teenager's face, a curly-haired, again carefully groomed, young adult face. I guess I saw all twenty-one birthday faces of my own son and tried to imagine six or seven more. HAPPY BIRTHDAY TO YOU - she sang her croaky, off-key song sitting beside his grave all alone. And I felt "Happy Birthday" must surely be the saddest song in the world to mothers like us. HAPPY BIRTHDAY, DEAR . . . HAPPY BIRTHDAY TO YOU . . .

Fay Harden
TCF, Tuscaloosa, AL

THE GRIEF OF OLDER PARENTS

It is difficult for society in general to understand the complexity of the loss of a child, no matter the age. Probably the two least understood losses are those at either end of the spectrum: the unsuccessful pregnancy, including stillbirth and death shortly after birth, and the loss of an adult child.

In the first case, they wonder why you grieve for someone they feel you didn't know, and in the second, they think that because the son or daughter no longer lived at home, wasn't a part of your everyday life, had a family of his or her own perhaps, that the pain of the death shouldn't be so bad. They seem not to understand that your children are a part of your life for all of your life, no matter how far away they may be.

Someone has reminded us that we do not love our children any more because they have lived long enough for the parents to watch them grow and develop. It is also important to realize that the older children aren't loved any less. You continue to love them and to develop new relationships with them. It is so frustrating for older parents to have poured all that time, effort and love into the rearing and shaping of a child; to have done a good job and had the time to see the end result; to have been able to like and enjoy the decent, worthwhile adult who has emerged and who is now a part of two relationships, that of parent/child and friend/friend. They have then lost both of those relationships.

Even if the older child has turned out not to be all that the parents hoped for and has caused unhappines with, for example, his alcoholism, the parents are still very much involved in this child's problems and escapades. Worrying about him and being a part of his support system becomes a way of life, and if this child dies, suddenly they are at a loss for a center in their life. They love him, no matter what his shortcomings, and they grieve for his loss as well.

As parents age, role reversals often develop between them and their adult children. After years of being responsible, in-charge people, as they age, they go from "What will happen to my children if something happens to me?" to "What will happen to me if something happens to my children?" The child becomes a large part of the older parent's security blanket, and they rely on him for comfort. The parents are reassured, thinking that when either of them dies, a child will be there to care for the one who is left.

Imagine a situation where the mother, who is widowed and in her 60's or 70's, now relies on her son, in his 40's or 50's, to help with her financial decisions, the upkeep of her home, and any problems she may have with her car, among other things. If she has health problems, he will see that she gets the proper medical care and whatever financial assistance he is able to offer. He may have already assured her of a place in his home should the need arise. Suddenly, this child dies. Fear and insecurity become a real part of the mother's life, as though she were a helpless, young child whose parents have died.

Some adult children, on the other hand, never leave home. Older, retired parents now find their daily life revolves around the routine comings and goings of this adult child. When he dies, the parents are cast adrift with no anchor, just as surely as parents of younger, terminally ill children after the death. What do you do with all of your time now that the hub of your universe is no longer there? All reasons for functioning seem to disappear.

If there are grandchildren left from this adult child who died, the grandparents now have to try and maintain a good relationship with the surviving in-law, hoping that efforts on the part of the son or daughter-in-law to begin a new life won't include cutting off all relationships with the old. Keeping in touch, but not intruding, can be tricky, particularly if there was not an especially good relationship between the grandparents and the in-law before the death. If the grandparents are denied access to their grandchildren, that is another great loss for them.

Most parents, no matter the age, will tell you they would have gladly taken their child's place in death, but older parents have inordinate amounts of survival guilt to deal with. What right do they, who have lived a long full life, have to be alive when their child is dead? "It should be me," they will tell you with great sadness.

A large part of survival after the death of a child is being able to motivate yourself to reinvest in life. If you aren't able to accomplish this after an appropriate length of time, you don't fare as well as those who can. If most of your life is behind you, as in the case of the older parents, they, who have already known a thousand little deaths over the years, have other losses of family and friends staring them in the face, as well as having to deal with their own mortality. Some of these parents, with age, aren't as mobile as they once were, so it is difficult for them to take advantage of any new interests that are available to them in their efforts to survive. Motivitation, then, though not impossible, certainly becomes more difficult. Older parents, like younger parents, are told that time will heal. The older parents answer, "But I don't have that much time." Therein lies the larger part of the problem with adjustment and reinvestment.

As you begin to understand the enormity of the loss of older parents, it is once again brought home that there is no good way or age to lose a child - just different ways and ages, and all of them hard.

Mary Cleckley
TCF, Atlanta, GA

CHAPTER VI

SITUATIONS CAN COMPLICATE THE GRIEF FOR A CHILD

Grief casts a sharper edge
on every day
and deepens all the shadows
in your life.

For you, whose grief is not
one grief alone,
those shadows have
the sharpest edge of all.

Because the grief
besieging you tonight
restores again
too many other sorrows,
the disappointments buried
in your heart.

Grief asks so many questions,
answers few —
grief takes away your patience
and your peace.

For you, whose grief meant
losing everything,
those questions have
the sharpest edge of all . . .

There is but half an answer
weeping in the silence:
Find comfort and endure.
Remember love.
And wait.

Sascha

MARRIAGE PROBLEMS

THE BEREAVED MARRIAGE

Before the death of a child, in an intact marriage both contribute to a mutually satisfying relationship. The following are areas of sharing before the death and where lack of sharing occurs afterwards:

Before, in family activities, couples shared what happened during the day, etc. After the death, they may have an initial sharing regarding the funeral and everything relating to the child, but not to them as a couple. Emotional support was a balancing act before the death. Often there is no emotional support afterwards, because each is so wrapped up in individual grief. People in grief become introspective—a typical thought is how am I going to go on? Before the death there was mutual concern for each other's well-being; afterwards the concern is turned inward. While before the death there was interest in each other's work, hobbies, and activities, afterwards nothing has meaning.

Males deal with grief differently from females because they are expected to be strong emotionally, to not show emotion, to not cry after the funeral. Society does not allow males to show anger over the death. As providers, men go back to work soon after and are away from where the memories are. They do not have as much time to think about what happened. As protectors, they may be feeling guilt. "Have I failed to protect my child in some way?" Also, there may be a feeling of wanting to protect the spouse by not being too emotional, by being "strong."

Men are more self-sufficient, especially in the emotional area. Men are not likely to share very well; this hurts their ability to grieve. Men hurt as much as women do, but usually do not show it until something triggers it. A man may talk about many things like sports and politics, but rarely is there someone with whom he can share his feelings. Men escape to the job, to outside activities. It is hard to find someone with whom to share feelings. Men do not usually recognize that it is all right to feel depressed.

Society says it is all right for a woman to cry and to talk about the loss. Women usually have a network with other women, although some of those making up the network may drop the woman because of not being able to face what has happened. Women set the tone for the family. When in grief, her responses set the tone for the family atmosphere and can be devastating. Because women are the primary child-caring persons, the mother may be the one feeling guilty because she had responsibility for the child's everyday care. Women are given more prescriptions for tranquilizers than men because of doctors' attitudes.

How do couples reconcile these variables? What can they do to lessen the impact? Men should take it easy regarding outside activities. Emphasis should be placed on getting into the business of grieving, even isolating oneself at times to be able to grieve. Men should find someone with whom to talk, preferably another bereaved father. Don't choose a woman because a man is too vulnerable emotionally and an unhealthy situation could develop. Men are "shaky" on accepting a group experience. If anger is what a man feels, he should express it by channeling it into something physical—be angry at something, not at a person. Daily exercise that is appropriate for the individual is another way of channeling aggression. Men should make a concerted effort to learn how to cry. Crying is a natural response; tear ducts have a natural purpose. Find a catalyst—a photo of your child, an article of clothing—anything that will make you cry. No one else need know about the crying if you go into another room.Some men find it takes much time before they feel free to cry, but once they do, it is then easier to continue to cry in private.

The woman in the bereaved couple should remember that she needs friends, especially other bereaved mothers. She should schedule time away from her job if she is a working mother, if nothing more than a flexible coffee break schedule. Nonworking mothers should use a baby sitter and plan time away from the usual environment. It is vital to nurture yourself. Physical exercise helps overcome depression and anger. Ask for help if you need it. If someone says, "What can I do?" give them something to do —shop, baby sit, clean house, write notes, something that will help you; it will also be good for the volunteer.

Until a death occurs, husband and wife behavior patterns within a family are predictable; afterwards, they are different. In the new husband-wife relationships don't try too much too fast. Drop expectations; be patient with each other. Respect how the other grieves and his timetable for doing it; no two people grieve exactly the same way or at the same pace.

If one spouse does not show grief, it does not mean memories are forgotten. Spend time together even if you have to schedule it. Each spouse is a reminder of the loss; for this reason they may even avoid each other. There may be feelings of guilt and conflict over sex. Usually one partner is ready and the other is not. Sex is a happy experience, yet often there is guilt for allowing yourself to feel good when your child is dead. Therefore, resume slowly and with patience. It is important to be able to say, "I am angry about what happened to our child, but it does not mean I love you any less."

Adapted from an article by
Bill and Barbara Schatz
TCF, Bothell, WA

TO MY HUSBAND

Your tears flow within your heart,
Mine flow down my cheeks.
Your anger lies with thought and movements,
Mine gallops forward for all to see.
Your despair shows in your now dull eyes,
Mine shows in line after written line.
You grieve over the death of your son,
I grieve over the death of my baby.
But we're still the same, still one,
Only we grieve at different times
Over different memories and at different lengths.
Yet we both realize
The death of our child.

Pam Burden
TCF, Augusta, GA

DOING TOO WELL

He told me that he had called because he was concerned about his wife. It had been five months since their child died and she wasn't doing well. I asked him what she was doing that bothered him, and he told me she was crying a great deal, wanted to talk about their child much of the time, wasn't sleeping well (was up a good part of the night wandering around, as a matter of fact), wanted to go to the cemetery almost every day, spent a lot of time looking at the child's pictures, and didn't want to change anything in "the" room.

And when I asked how he was doing, he told me he was doing fine, was working 13 or 14 hours a day (hadn't always worked that much, but had been for the past two or three months), said he didn't need to talk about their child or look at the pictures because he had put it all behind him, had accepted it and he thought she would be better if she would do the same. Sleep? Well, he slept fine. He'd found a few drinks before he went to bed, plus a tranquilizer when he awakened in the middle of the night and more of each on the weekend, helped him quite a bit.

Now, if she's doing "poorly" and he's doing so "fine," why is it, do you suppose, that I keep worrying about him?

Mary Cleckley
TCF, Atlanta, GA

A LESSON IN GRIEF

When our son was killed, I remember thinking through the haze of pain that this most horrifying of life experiences would somehow bring us closer. Sharing the loss of a child created and loved by both of us for twenty years would surely deepen the bond between us. I was in for a surprise.

We clung almost blindly to each other until the shock began to give way to ugly reality. As we each moved to our individual pattern of grieving, differences began to emerge. I felt like a time bomb about to explode. I needed desperately to talk about our son. My husband refused to verbalize his feelings and became angry at my overtures. I stopped trying to communicate.

This was beyond my comprehension. Where was my helpmate, my best friend? I felt rejected, unloved and terribly alone. Anger overwhelmed me as I bitterly realized that I wasn't going to be able to share my grieving with the person who meant the most to me in the world. I knew that many marriages fail after the death of a child. Dear God, how could we possibly survive an additional tragedy?

We attended a few Compassionate Friends meetings and then I continued alone. The gentle acceptance of others who had lost a child permitted me to talk or cry without guilt. Our problem was definitely not unique, many other parents expressed similar frustrations. So many couples experience marital difficulty after the death of a child that it is now considered the norm. We weren't going crazy; just because our grieving styles were different didn't mean that our whole marriage would fall apart. My anger began to dissipate as I slowly faced the fact that I had been placing unrealistic expectations on my husband. Hurting at least as much as I, he simply could not meet my needs for support.

We began to have some honest discussions, agreeing that we needed each other's nurturing in order to survive and find meaning in life. We learned to respect each other's feelings. We tried to please each other in little ways: a hug, a special meal, anything that expressed caring. Patience with each other smoothed over many rough moments. Time spent alone together was very healing. It took a conscious decision from both of us to try harder. Some days we didn't have any energy left when grief was particularly painful. It wasn't always easy as we still couldn't talk about our son for a long time.

Much later the knowledge that support had been there all along from my friends if I had only asked for it, saddened me. I had to admit that I simply had been too proud to reveal myself as a suffering person in need of help. I will be forever grateful to Compassionate Friends for being there with loving, open arms.

As I look back, ignorance of grief and the impact it can have on a marriage was the basis for our problems. But, in retrospect, how could we possibly have been prepared for the onslaught of paralyzing emotions that overwhelmed us? Anguish of this intensity can reveal a spouse you've never seen before. Deeply wounded, you will both be inevitably changed from the experience of losing a child. Understanding these simple facts would have helped immeasurably.

Pat Retzloff
TCF, Oshkosh, WI

IT'S OVER

And it's over!
Finally everyone has gone away
To turn their lives back on again
Like radios
Leaving us to talk too loudly
Trying to soak up the silence.

Sometimes I see you turn away
So that I won't see your tears
And we build this incredible wall
Of grief
First started with her empty chair.

I can't believe that I could ever be
So alone with you
Each of us guarding our pain
Jealously
As the last thing to hold of her.

And people said,
"You're so lucky to have each other."

Sue Borrowman
TCF, Winnepeg, Canada

WHEN PARENTS ARE SINGLE, DIVORCED OR WIDOWED

GRIEF AND THE SINGLE PARENT

The death of a child is an unanticipated, shocking, devastating event in any family. In the single-parent home, the death of a child or children can be more difficult than in the two-parent home. Families have a difficult enough time coping with this life passage - the added burden of making arrangements and paying expenses. When adults have gone through a life crisis like divorce, the stress of dealing with the necessary arrangements presents another barrier on the long road of restructuring the single's life.

We may be on speaking terms with the ex-spouse and that is helpful to a point. Those who are not on speaking terms are faced with even greater stress. The emotional ties that at one time connected us to this lost child are no longer present, yet to many it points up the hurt of the past. Survivors search for something or someone to blame. (In two-parent homes, divorce is up to 80% after the loss of a child.) Widows/widowers are confronted with compounded griefs. Unfortunately, most of us do not get through life with only one crisis. Dealing with the past rekindles the hurts of the past.

As parents, we would be well advised by the legal system and counselors to make an effort to be amicable and/or courteous to the ex-spouse. The fact remains that legally, as parents, we are responsible for the minor children. Insurance policies may be in the name of the ex-spouse; papers must be signed. Grandparents, siblings, relatives and friends are also in grief. We must deal with them all. Who can our remaining children turn to if not us for guidance through these crises?

If you have a companion who has suffered this loss, be patient. If you are the parent who has lost a child, ask your companion to be patient with you. The grief process is longer than we knew it would be. To the non-bereaved parent, the grief process is longer than you can know. This life passage is not something we want for any of you. The death of a marriage is not comparable to the death of a child. Often the widow/widower or the divorced person may remarry. The loss of a child is not a void which can be filled. There are entirely different emotions to be dealt with.

Many of us survive but will forever have emotional scars. Stand by us and we will be forever grateful. Many of you have done that for me. Unfortunately, for several, I am now trying to stand by you in your loss. In our singleness, as a friend, you are invaluable.

Jacque Stockhausen
TCF, St. Louis, MO

GRIEVING ALONE: A SINGLE PARENT'S EXPERIENCE

When a single parent experiences grief over the death of a child, there are several areas that make it an especially difficult time. The purpose of this article is to point them out and to provide some suggestions that may help. Bereaved couples who find their grief is driving them apart and placing a strain on their marriage face many of the same problems, and they may also find these suggestions helpful.

Some brief background: In April of 1982, my only child, Aaron, died at age 19. An avid runner and healthy outdoorsman, he was kicked in his abdomen by a horse. He was hospitalized for a month, courageously fighting an infection, but died during a fifth surgery. Aaron and I had always been very close. I had raised him by myself since he was three. His death was a devastating shock.

The following issues and dilemmas are among those I encountered that were different from those faced by the bereaved parent who is not alone.

1. A Strong Sense of Isolation. When your child dies the world seems to tumble around you. It feels particularly frightening to a single parent, for there's no partner to reach out and bridge the gap of isolation. We need others to help us balance our upside-down world, to encourage us to keep hanging on when it seems too unbearable.

Often the isolation becomes real after a few weeks of bereavement. Friends who've been supportive drift away, assuming someone else is checking on your well-being. Constantly taking the initiative to reach out for support is draining and tiring when you do it three times a week every week for months, and the pain and the need don't seem to lessen.

T.C.F. was a life saver for me. I knew that other members were available by phone, and willing to talk or listen. Just knowing that helped me ease that sense of isolation.

2. Inconsistency. As every hour of every day seemed like a challenge to "get through," the only person I knew I could depend on was me! Needing to be strong for myself at times seemed just too much. I longed for someone I could depend on to reassure me when I was feeling emotionally distraught. As assertive as I am, I found it impossible to ask for what I wanted most, one person to give one night a week just to spend time with me in my home. We could buy groceries for dinner and share the cooking, eat together. talk or watch TV or read, simply sharing time and space on a consistent basis.

But that didn't happen. I found that when I wanted company, I was expected to do something, go out to a restaurant, attend a concert, see a movie, because my friends felt I needed to "get out of the house." Being sociable and entertaining when you're dealing with fresh grief is very difficult, however. It's hard to think of anything but the child who died.

Those who have understanding relatives nearby can and should look to them for stability during the early months of grief. With family you can "just be." Close friends can be asked to fill this important role, too.

3. Sharing Emotions. Research shows that 25 percent of the stress from the loss of a loved one can be relieved by simply sharing with another person your thoughts, feelings, and ideas. But every time we, as singles, feel the need to express what's going on inside our minds and bodies, we have to seek someone out. Sometimes we don't have the emotional strength to even dial the phone. We dread finding that all our friends are busy or not home, knowing we may end up feeling more rejected than when we began.

Yet we need assistance in resolving important issues. For example, I felt guilty for eight months after Aaron's death that I hadn't stayed with my son the first night he was admitted to the hospital. I thought he might be alive today if I had stayed that first night. Finally I happened to share my feelings with a friend who stated that she felt it was the responsibility of the nurses and doctors. I'd not looked at it that way before, and it made my guilt feelings subside. Someone had helped me look at the situation from a different angle. We need others and people who'll listen are not always easy to find.

4. Sharing The Work. A single parent who has other children at home has a special burden. Not only is the parent grieving over the loss of a child, he or she must also go back to work for a living, try to maintain stability at home for the remaining children, and handle the normal, everyday household problems. Additionally, that parent must devote attention to the remaining children so they won't be emotionally "marred" because of the tragic situation. This seems too much to ask of anyone, yet many single parents do it day after day. I am very concerned about the long term effects created by this extra stress. These single parents need special support systems; for example, friends might volunteer to come in or take the children out occasionally to relieve the load.

5. Sharing The Special Memories. No one except you knows the special qualities that made your child unique. As a single parent, you have no one who remembers that child as you do and who can share those memories with you. If you have other children, you will be able to reminisce with them about those traits you all remember. I continue to share with others my son's unique qualities so they, and he, won't be forgotten. However, it requires so much explaining to those who didn't know him that the joys of sharing such memories are often lost.

To keep from doing this too often, which tends to bother others, I have used writing as a way to not let him be forgotten. Putting my memories of Aaron's humor, quiet presence, and other characteristics in print helps fulfill my need for continuity.

6. Support From The Opposite Sex. As we've learned, getting emotional support form a non-bereaved person is difficult enough; dating and seeking emotional support adds another level of stress.

Dates are supposed to be fun. Since I was in mourning, I explained to my date from the outset so he wouldn't expect a date who bubbled with joy. I was seldom in a light mood, but I did want to see men occasionally.

At first they'd be very understanding, but after a few dates they thought I "should be over it by now" (this during my first year of bereavement), and we'd part ways. Then I would feel abandoned again, compounding my sense of loss. I needed to feel important to someone, but I decided after a few such partings that I was not ready to be emotionally involved. In facing the pain of grief I had no energy left for building a new relationship that first year.

7. Making Decisions and Facing Major Events Alone. After Aaron's memorial service I was left with all the decisions. I sorted all his possessions, each article of clothing, letters and papers. I was the one who dealt with the dogs. I decided how and where to bury the ashes. Such tasks were grueling to face alone. I wanted someone to share the responsibility.

Each time a major event such as Mother's Day, Aaron's birthday, and Christmas arrived, I had to once again thumb through my address book to find someone who would talk it over with me and help me handle those difficult times.

8. The Need For Touch. My personal observation is that bereaved people have a strong need for touching and hugging. The contact not only feels good but can have a healing quality.

Being single means there's no spouse nearby to provide that gentle touch on the back or that consoling hug when the pain erupts. When you're single, you need to find other sources, like friends and relatives who know how to hug you and do so. Reach out to them often as you grieve. Some of my friends were "huggers" and one friend, a therapeutic masseuse, gave me a free massage once a week for that entire first year.

If you have surviving children, hug them often. You'll all benefit from it.

9. Grieving At Your Own Pace. The only benefit to grieving alone is that the single parent does not have to take into account a spouse's needs and feelings. We do not have to worry about disturbing another's sleep as we cry during the night or hold back our tears when our spouse's spirits are high.

10. Special Strengths. One of our assets is the strength we've gained during our struggles as single parents. We may never have discovered that inner strength if we had not been alone. Your special strength, plus the coping skills you've gained as a single parent, are valuable. You were strong enough to handle alone your job as parent; that knowledge can give you the courage you need to survive the grieving alone. And reaching out for others' support sometimes takes the most courage of all.

Kelly Osmont
TCF, Portland, OR

WHAT HAPPENS WHEN A CHILD DIES AND THE PARENTS ARE DIVORCED

No one can describe or understand the pain a parent feels when his child dies. Greater than the loss of a person's own parents, sibling or spouse is the overwhelming loss associated with the death of a child. No matter the age or circumstances accompanying the child's death—the pain is excruciating.

According to the National Center for Health Statistics, well over 100,000 children die each year either accidentally or through disease. Presently, one out of two marriages end in divorce in the United States. In 1985, there were one million divorces in this country. Consequently, a new dilemma facing society is the death of a child in a divorced family.

Psychologists, physicians, members of the clergy, and others who deal with the bereaved do not know how to counsel the bereaved divorced family. There are no rules, literature, or courses addressing this issue. Everyone is virtually impotent in handling this special kind of tragedy.

The distress confronting the divorced family may be more intense, confusing and difficult than that of the intact family for a myriad of reasons. In some cases, the divorced parents' grief is exacerbated by guilt, blame, resentment and possible hostilities resulting from the divorce and/or either partner's remarriage. Let us look at some of the other problems that accompany the death of a child in a divorced family.

CUSTODY. Usually one parent will have custody of the child. Even if it is shared custody, the child will likely be with only one parent at the time of death. Regardless in whose care the child was at the time of death, blame and guilt operate in tandem. Although it is a natural reaction when someone is hurting to blame someone else, this syndrome is more intensely felt in divorced families.

In one case, a child was visiting her father for the weekend. The father was in constant phone contact with the mother regarding a diabetic complication. Finally, the mother received a call stating that the father was at the emergency room to have the daughter evaluated, but the caller reassured her that everything was fine. Upon arrival at the hospital the mother was informed by nurses that they "were trying to resuscitate the child." The child was not revived. The mother never spoke to her child again. In this particular case, the mother, against her better judgment, let her daughter go for the weekend. Not only did she blame herself, but she felt rage at her ex-husband for not alerting her to the gravity of the situation.

This is not to say that some intact families don't have to deal with irresponsibility and blame. Carelessness can happen to anyone. Hopefully, the anger and blame will pass for the intact family either through time or counseling or both. The divorced family would hardly seek joint counseling to cope with their anger and the resulting blame and resentment. As one parent stated, "Because of divorce, the lonely is more lonely."

OTHER CHILDREN. Is there an amicable solution in dealing with other children in the family? Besides natural siblings, the divorced family may also include stepchildren and half brothers and sisters.

Where do these children stay during the planning stages of the pending funeral? Which parent has the right to them if both parents want them? Who will see their pain and grief, their guilt and their confusion and anxiety?

In one family of seven children from separate marriages, the children chose to stay with the father and stepmother after their brother died. Although they preferred being with the father and stepmother, they may have experienced guilt over not choosing to stay with their mother.

FUNERAL ARRANGEMENTS. The complexities involved with funeral arrangements are immense. Naturally, funeral decisions are extremely emotional. But for the divorced family who may not be on speaking terms, the task is seemingly unsurmountable.

By law, the funeral home accords the legal guardian the privilege of his choice regarding all details of the burial service. If the divorced parents are not amicable, the custodial parent alone makes the final decisions - whether it be the type of casket, opened or closed, selection of music, cemetery lot and location, choice of seating arrangements, or any of the other myriad of details.

It is not uncommon for divorced parents to quarrel over any details of the service, including who will select the casket spray. One might want a single pink rose, while the other prefers a $500 arrangement. Emotions run high at this time, and generally the funeral director will prefer not to be a referee. One funeral home that handles 2,000 funerals per year stated that about 50% of the divorced families are amicable about the arrangements and the remaining 50% are quarrelsome and even combative. Due to the circumstances, each family reacts differently and no one solution works for everyone.

At the funeral, assuming the divorced parents will not be sitting together but instead with their own spouse, friend, or family member, where do the children sit? Who will decide this, and how many hurt feelings will result?

In the case of the family mentioned above, all six remaining children sat with the father on one side of the funeral chapel, while the mother, her friends and close relatives, sat on the other side. The private area of the chapel, normally reserved for the family, was closed completely, thereby avoiding any arguments over seating privileges.

The majority of parents do not have an accomodating relationship after divorce. Although they may say, "Little David or Kimberly would want us to be at peace today," the facade is weak and could likely crack at any given moment.

and almost impossible in divorced families. The way people react to bereavement varies tremendously depending on personalities, the circumstances surrounding the child's death, and what each feels regarding the divorce.

THE CHILD'S BELONGINGS. The intact family never has to face this particular problem - the disposition of the child's personal effects between two parents in two separate homes. Although the greatest portion of a child's possessions will not be the subject of an argument, there may be one or two very special articles that mean a lot to one or both parents. Perhaps it is a stuffed animal, a certain picture, a senior ring, but both parents cannot possess it now. With thoughtfulness, consideration and a desire to be flexible, even this most difficult decision can be managed by the divorced parents.

One thoughtful mother xeroxed a copy of the guest book which she received from the funeral home and presented it to her ex-husband, along with a scrapbook of her son's life in pictures and other memorabilia.

PRIVILEGE AND RIGHT OF A PARENT. This area deals with rights of a parent to the privileges accorded the bereaved. In many cases a parent who has been estranged for years shows up at the hospital or funeral home and expects special treatment because he is a parent. Nevermind that he left the child physically and emotionally abandoned for an extended period of time.

A certain phenomenon happens at the time of the child's death. Like at a son's or daughter's wedding, the absent parent arrives to take his or her place among the wedding party and expects all the privileges accorded to the father or mother of the bride or groom. The parent who has remained active in the child's life may be openly hostile to the prodigal parent and make statements like, "What gives him the right to come in here after treating her like he did for so many years?" "How dare she think she can just show up and expect everyone to be solicitous of her feelings."

These stressful situations and many others arise when a child dies and the parents are divorced. Under the heaviest duress they have ever experienced, divorced parents must find a way to resolve all the issues facing them. Perhaps by making the public aware of some of these perplexing problems, solutions will be forthcoming . . . solutions that will soothe the inexhaustible pain facing the bereaved divorced parent.

Savannah Lowe
TCF, Friendswood, TX

WHEN THERE IS A STEPPARENT INVOLVED

THE LOSS OF A CHILD NOT YOUR OWN

For as many reasons as there are people on earth, parents may have children who are not their own. The love of "another" parent may be as deep as that of the natural parent, but it is different. They may be as protective and supportive as a natural parent. Their relationship with the child who has died may have been very close. The child may not have made a distinction between natural and other parents, and the loss of a child for "adoptive" parents is in many respects as devastating an experience for stepparents as it is for natural parents.

The anguish and grief are deep, the outrage and questions as pronounced, the frustrations and feeling of helplessness are as real as for the natural parent. That the feelings and pain are somewhat slanted by the difference can bring a balance of support that is missing and has to be rebuilt in total, for natural parents. But the struggles to cope with the loss are as hard, the road back often as long for those of us who have a stepchild, as they are for natural parents.

We have something that approaches a "painful acceptance" in a much shorter time than would otherwise be expected or possible for natural parents. The road back may not be as long, the valley of despair may not be as deep, but still they must be traveled. I will miss "my son" for as long as I live. I will always hold close the memories I have. Yet, it is different, different in a way that is a godsend to my wife, different in a way that gives her a greater degree of support and gives me a better purpose than I had before. We are, because of our loss, closer in many ways, yet more distant because of the difference. Some things I cannot share. I can only support. Some pains I cannot ease, but I can be very patient. Some tears I cannot stop, but I can be the shoulder that she needs. There are times that a shoulder is all I can be. Thank God, a shoulder is all she needs.

From the Sacramento Valley Newsletter

REFLECTIONS OF A STEPPARENT

I watched my mate go through pure hell.
And I felt helpless, useless, and
sometimes . . . invisible.

Other times - I stood strong while
Bearing the brunt of my love's anger
That lashed out at the world -
As an angry God would open the heavens
With roaring thunder and lightning.

I was accused of not understanding
And surely . . . I could not.

I felt heavy pain for my stepchild,
The one I took as my own.
I grieved for the good times we had together,
The tugs at my heart that always
Pierced through any resentments.

The guilt weighed heavily on my shoulders
For the times we didn't communicate
And I wondered if . . .
I could have made it better.

At the funeral home, I felt even a pang of . . .
Yes . . . jealousy
Toward the natural parent of my beloved stepchild,
Knowing that they and my mate shared
A private room from the past
That I could never . . . ever . . . enter.

Life must go on . . . this day-to-day existence,
But things are different now.

I offer my support
As I see eyes staring off into
A distant land.
I hold a hand
And kiss away the teardrops.

With an added sorrow, I wonder
If my love will return to me or
Stay in that far-off land . . . forever.
For deep in my heart I know that
This tragedy will bring us closer together
Or tear us completely apart.

Peggi Hull
TCF, Houston-Bay Area Chapter

STEPPARENTS GRIEVE TOO

Stepparents deal with a unique type of grief. If both parents are living and are part of funeral arrangements, we might feel very much apart from the planning and the gathering of friends and relatives. We need to share this feeling of isolation with someone. We loved the deceased child and had our own special relationship with him. Much like with the subject of death, many people feel very awkward in situations where a divorced couple are together in the same room. We must deal with this, as well as our own grief and that of our other family members.

We are not abnormal because we need to grieve. We have that right just as we accepted the right to love and care for our stepchildren. We need to talk about our feelings with family, friends, and members of TCF. We belong at TCF meetings. It is normal if our spouses question our grief. When someone is hurting badly, they find it difficult to believe anyone else can be hurting that badly too. We must be aware of the opportunity to share our grief with our spouses and families, but not get into ridiculous discussions concerning who is grieving the most. What each family member is feeling and when they feel it IS NORMAL FOR THEM.

Unfortunately, the Cinderella syndrome of stepparents carries over into real life. Unless a person is a stepparent, they sometimes have no idea of the bond that can develop between a stepparent and child. Many of us made a much more concerted effort to love our spouses' children than we did to love our natural children. We not only learned to love our stepchildren, but also learned to understand them and become more objective than the natural parents. Our grief is very natural and we certainly have the right to grieve. Just because we weren't present when the child was born doesn't lessen the degree of hurt.

We must rise above petty jealousy and accept that the child's natural parents may be drawn together when their child dies. Each natural parent will be suffering guilt that may include "Our child would be still alive if our marriage had survived." This feeling may last for several months, particularly if the death was unexpected. Discussions with other divorced parents at TCF can help diminish this feeling, but it is natural and can affect us and our marriages - IF WE LET IT. We are not the best qualified, nor are we emotionally capable to counsel our spouses. Hopefully, a trained counselor or member of the clergy can be of assistance.

As difficult as it may be, we should not only understand the need for the natural parents to spend time together, but by encouraging this, we may also strengthen our marriages and eliminate problems that may develop at a future time. Understanding is vital as we deal with our own grief and that of our families. The need for the natural parents to reminisce about the past is natural and healthy. We should not consider this a rejection by our spouses and other step-children. It is difficult to feel isolated from our family, but we can't allow hurt pride to surface. The degree of guilt our spouses feel will have a direct bearing on the need for contact with the other natural parent and the degree of isolation we encounter. We must also be prepared to help our spouses if they are rejected by their former spouses. OUR GOAL SHOULD BE . . . BE PART OF THE HEALING, NOT AN ADDITIONAL PROBLEM.

Whether we feel capable or not, whether we feel up to it or not, the other children may turn to us for guidance, support and love. We must remember that adults and children grieve differently and at different times, just as mothers and fathers do. If the surviving children are worried about their natural parent's grief, they need to discuss this concern. We should be prepared. We also must help to make the surviving children feel important by taking an interest in their everyday activities. While we are wondering if our lives can possibly go on after losing a child, lives of the surviving children do continue and they get back to normal activities and relationships much faster than we do. While grieving for the dead child, we can't allow the surviving children to feel guilty because they are still alive. OUR ROLES AS PARENTS MAY INCREASE DRAMATICALLY.

Jay Brady,
TCF, Omaha, NE

WHEN ONLY OR ALL CHILDREN DIE

ON LOSS OF ALL CHILDREN

We knew how it felt to lose one child, and now how do we feel when we lose another child, or in our case, all of our children? Our loss is devastating. We try to take one day at a time and do the best we can that day. We talk with understanding and compassionate friends. We read all the books we can on grief and grief recovery. We pray for strength and courage. Our faith tells us our children are safe in God's Everlasting Arms, but our hearts tell us we want our children here with us now.

We know we never lose the love we have for our children, and the love we shared with them will always be in our hearts. We don't lose that love. We just miss their presence so much. If we could only hug or kiss them one more time. If we could just hear them say, "Hey, Mom" or "Hey, Dad" once more. If we could receive one more Mother's or Father's Day card. If we could only tell them "we love you" one more time.

It has been said when we lose our parents, we lose a part of our past, but when we lose a child, we lose a part of our future. When we lose all our children, we are losing all our future concerning them. We feel different or set apart from our friends and others who have children because we no longer have our children in common as we once did. We begin to wonder what role or identity we have in life anymore. We have experienced parenthood, but we are no longer active parents. Our hopes of being in-laws are gone, as are our hopes and dreams of becoming grandparents. Many of the roles we had anticipated will never be realized. All of us feel a little of ourselves will live on through our children, but when all of your children die, you lose your dreams of immortality.

When we lose a child, it feels like an amputation. A part of ourselves is missing. With each child we lose, it is like another amputation, like being torn apart with many pieces missing and many chunks taken out, and not much left of ourselves. We wonder what it will be like as we grow older without the children we had counted on having with us in our old age.

Losing all our children might be described as "A Lonely Road." We find ourselves traveling on a lonely and unfamiliar road we've never been on before and we've lost our road map. We come to an intersection that leads off in about three different directions. We don't know which road to take, have no idea which way to turn. Our lives have no certain direction and we don't know where the road ahead leads. The road we are on now isn't the road we planned to travel. This road is lonely, rocky, and uphill with a lot of bumps and rough places. We feel we don't have the answers now, but we search and struggle to find the right road to take. We will find that road, and where it leads will be our choice in the end.

Excerpts from an article
by Delores Watson
TCF, Springfield, MO

THE DEATH OF AN ONLY OR ALL CHILDREN

In dealing with parents who have experienced the death of an only or all their children, I have found the same underlying feelings of never fully resolving the death of their child and never really accepting their lives without children. Their sense of guilt or anger seems heightened and their withdrawal from friends, family and society is more complete than that of parents with surviving children.

As with any parental bereavement, there is the empty feeling of not being a parent anymore. But recovery is complicated because we have no other children alive and, therefore, we are not allowed to be a parent. We question, "Am I still a mother?" or "Am I still a father?" There is a strong response of caring very little about ourselves because the whole purpose of our lives is gone. We may ignore our health, retreat from people, and never fully recover to the point of reinvesting our love and energies in our future.

The following are some of the ways that the grief after the death of an only child or all children differs from the grief of those who have surviving children.

There is no one to "parent." There are no other children for whom to do the things we have been in training to do. There is acute frustration in not being able to do what we know we can do - parent.

The loss is complete for those who have no hope of other children, or for single parents who can never have the same mixture of a child with that child's other parent.

We find we have a lot of time and energy and no direction for it. Our spouse, the dog, the cat, a foster child, baby sitting, or having the nieces and nephews over does not compensate for our loss of directed energies.

Our physical space - the house, the car, or perhaps the shopping cart - is not filled with anyone. It is quiet and sometimes the sound of that silence is deafening.

If we cannot have another child, we have lost our future. We may never have grandchildren and the questions arise, "Who will take care of me in my old age?" or "What do I have to look forward to?"

Reactions from other people may be different. Do they still regard me as a parent? Our place in life has changed and other people perceive that. When we are faced with the question of "How many children do you have?" it is more difficult for those of us who have no other living children. The question really becomes "Am I still a parent?"

We may have a tendency to idolize the lost child or children beyond what is natural for the grief process because we have no other children to remind us of what is normal for a child. We have no one else with whom to make a comparison.

As the years go by, concern increases that no one around us will ever have known our child or children and talking about them will become more difficult or unnatural in this company. How will we express ourselves in ten, fifteen, or twenty years? Who will want to know about our dead child or children when the people we know will probably be grandparents by that time? We question if after this length of time we are still a parent at all.

When children die at different times, it seems the support diminishes with each loss. Generally, people seem to feel that by now we know how to handle the loss because we have been through it before . . . that perhaps losing all our children blurs the loss of an individual child.

The death of an only child may prompt a feeling of negating the usefulness of several years of the past and we might feel "What a waste of time, energy and love to have it taken away." Sometimes we feel "Was it really worth it?"

What we have worked to accomplish and accumulate in our lives can no longer be left as an inheritance for our children.

We have all heard that time will heal all wounds. I believe we need to take control of that time and change the passive waiting into active doing.

We need to seek new outlets for the energy we formerly put into parenting. We might find it helpful to use others who have never been parents as role models or resource guides for building our future. We need to keep a growing edge on life as we reluctantly turn our eyes from the past to the future. We can do it more easily if we seek new interests, new knowledge, new friendships,and, most of all, if we seek a new life. Piece by piece we can put the puzzle back together, finding the completeness which comes with total reinvestment and redirection of our energies and love.

Excerpts from an article
by Edie Kaplan
TCF, Broward Co./Greater Ft. Lauderdale

THE SECOND-TIME BEREAVED

OUR CHILDREN DID EXIST

I've lost two children, I hear myself say,
And the person I'm talking to just turns away.

Now why did I tell them, I don't understand.
It wasn't for sympathy or to get a helping hand.

I just want them to know we've lost something dear.
I want them to know that our children were here.

They left something behind which no one can see.
They made just two people into a family.

So, if I've upset you, I'm sorry as can be.
You'll have to forgive me, I could not resist.

I just wanted you to know that our children did exist.

Betty Schreiber
TCF, Ashtabula, OH

THE SECOND-TIME BEREAVED

Very few of us in TCF have lost more than one child. We know the excruciating pain of losing that child, but what of the parent who has lost two or more children? One of TCF's greatest assets is in seeing others like ourselves. We know we are not alone and that others have made it through this horrendous experience - thus we are given hope. But the parent who loses the second child (or God forbid, the third or fourth) cannot feel the commonness that the others in the group share. They are experiencing the unthinkable, and rarely is there another parent in the group who has experienced this. The real value of TCF is lost to them.

Unfortunately, in the TCF groups I have seen the same things happen to the second-loss parents that happen to the bereaved parent in general society. They are avoided, or at least they are not given the extra support they need. Just as the non-bereaved do not know what to say to us, neither do we know what to say to this parent. It is possible that we have the unconscious fear that we, too, might lose a second child; as if by being with or talking to a second-time bereaved parent, it could happen to us also. Another possibility is that seeing a parent who is bereaved for the second time might, in a sense, minimize our own loss for us, and we are uncomfortable with that.

When we lose the first child, we are blessedly ignorant of what we will experience in the months ahead. As a result, we don't project ahead to what we will feel; therefore, that stress is not added. But the parent who has already experienced the death of one child knows what it is like and what is ahead of them. This could greatly increase the anxiety and fear, in addition to the present grief.

Most parents who lose two children lose them at separate times rather than both children dying at the same time. This creates the problem of reliving the experiences and emotions of the first child's death, while at the same time going through the second child's death. The death, the funeral, and every new experience that occurs will bring back vivid memories of the first child's death, and that experience is felt again. With the reliving of the past grief comes comparisons which further complicate this grief.

Not only will the parents themselves compare the deaths and experiences, but others will also. This could lead to even more stress for the parent, especially if the second death was not an "acceptable" one. If the death was from an illness or accident, the parents are supported and cared for to a greater degree than if the death was by suicide. Of course, the reverse is true and if the second death is the "acceptable" one, that may lead to increased support for the parent. Certainly we do hope this does not happen in TCF, but we must be aware that it does happen in general society and the second-time bereaved might need our additional support.

Another reason the second-time bereaved may receive less support is because somehow people have the idea that if you went through this one time, the second time will be easier. We know a child's death never becomes easier. Each death is different.

It is possible that the death of the second child will cause the normal intensity of parental grief to be even greater than the first time. The first-time bereaved feel that as terrible as their grief has been, they have survived or are surviving, and the feeling is that some day this will be over and that they can live their lives once more in peace. They generally feel confident that they will not have to go through this again, but the second-time bereaved parent knows it does happen again. If they have other children, they fear that another one could die. There is no consolation in survival for them. They might well feel helplessly trapped in a web of children's deaths. Hope for a better future is not so certain for the second-time bereaved. They may experience even deeper feelings of hopelessness and futility than the first-time bereaved parent does.

Another issue for the second-time bereaved may be in missing the children in different ways. Each child was unique and played his or her own part in the parent's life, and what is missed about each may be totally different. Differences in the children may create additional pain and stress for the parent if, as in some cases, the one child was a loving and lovable one and the other was was not.

Sometimes for a number of reasons there is an unspoken sense of relief in one of the deaths that was not a part of the other death. This could add considerable guilt to the parent's grief, and frequently the parent will not speak out of the relief for fear of censure by others. Thus they suffer this guilt alone.

It is hard to know what to say to a parent who has lost more than one child. The loss of one child is devastating. The thought of losing two children is unthinkable, but unthinkable as it may be, it does in fact happen. It is important that we all be aware of the unique problems that accompany the multiple losses and that we sincerely extend our hand to these unfortunate parents. We may not know exactly what they are going through, nor know what to say, but we can be willing to be with them, listen to them and support them as best we can. It takes a little extra effort.

Margaret Gerner
TCF, St. Louis, MO

HOW DOES IT FEEL?

How does it feel to have two gone?
Do you know what it feels like to have to get through saying two names and circumstances in the TCF circle at the beginning of the meeting? People mentally, if not verbally, click their tongues.
You think you've got it bad,
A setting apart from the group?
I didn't want to be a part of your group anyway, to be a member of a loser's group.
So there.
Does losing our two cancel out your one? You look for signs of me having a better-than-thou demeanor, of wanting a brighter and bigger medal of distinction. But you can't find any signs of that. I don't want to complain how bad it is lest you feel that I'm saying that your pain does not measure up to mine.
How about if we agree not to compete?
Listen to my pain, I'll listen to yours.
I feel shaken to the quick, devastated to the core.
Some days I feel I will break up into a bundle of pieces lying on the floor. How about you? How does it feel?
It feels barren.
I realize that without intending to, I pretend that they are still here . . . they're just not home right now.

I get by because I believe that if they had lived longer, they only would have suffered more. I go on in defiance of despair and hopelessness (These two uglies I try to keep at bay because they're too ugly and scary for me to let them stay uninvited for very long. They are like a flood that rises up to the closed door of my home, only to seep under the threshold.) because I believe in their eternal salvation.
Say I only believe that because I need to— but I think you're wrong.
I will continue to make the best I can out of my life, because to do otherwise would be to say theirs counted for nothing.
Well, they taught us how to live.
But every now and then the cracks show through my armor and I go crashing again to the floor, breaking into a hundred pieces like a piece of crystal glass.
But when the darkness leaves the night and I shimmer in the light,
I see rainbows cast in every direction.
And I "trace the rainbow through the rain. and feel the promise is not vain . . . that life shall endless be."
Please hold my hand. Do you have it? I have yours.

Jean Geuder
TCF, St. Louis, MO

THE DEATH OF DISABLED CHILDREN

THE DEATH OF DISABLED CHILDREN

Although it's been 10 years since my son Daniel's death, I occasionally encounter a memento of his life - a crayoned letter drawn on one of his possessions. As I look at it, it seems to me symbolic of Daniel. Of course, all children are special. Some, however, through birth, accident, or illness, are slightly less than perfect. That slight difference makes the death of those children unique.

Daniel was dyslexic. The crayoned letters marking his belongings were a part of the logical illogicalness of his life. The letter itself was made from right to left and from bottom to top. When finished, however, it looked "normal" just like Daniel himself.

It is the painful struggle with life that makes the death of a disabled child unique. While the parents miss the child, they probably do not miss the disability. Because of this, they feel guilty. For example, I wanted Daniel back desperately; I did not want the learning disability. Because the disability and Daniel were inseparable, I felt guilty. I also felt relief over no longer having to deal with the dyslexia and its emotional effects upon Daniel. I felt guilty about that as well.

Life with Daniel was a paraphrase of the beginning of ***A Tale of Two Cities.*** *He was the best of children; he was the worst of children. I cried myself to sleep missing the boy who expressed sensitivity to others. Often he shared his special blanket with someone not feeling well.*

One Mother's Day present was a promise not to step on my injured feet all day. Yet I was relieved to be free of the boy who often threw tantrums so severe they persisted until he fell into deep sleep. One tantrum had resulted in his biting my arm then backing across the room still clenching my flesh in his teeth. I longed for my caring son; I was relieved to no longer fear the raging one. Such strongly ambivalent emotions complicate the grief process.

Adding to the conflicting emotions of loss and relief is anger. The parents feel frustrated and betrayed by the fact that their child's continual struggle was in vain. A friend expressed this feeling for me when she said, "If there were only to be eight years for Daniel, why did they have to be like that?"

Another source of difficulty for parents of handicapped children is blame assessment. Whether the disability is the result of heredity, illness, or injury, the parents may have felt responsible. The death of the child adds to existing guilt or reawakens former guilt which further complicates the grief process.

Because of their many problems, handicapped children required an enormous amount of their parents' time and concern. Suddenly, with the death of the child, there is a huge void. Nothing can fill it. Yet, the longer the void remains, the more acutely the parents feel the loss of the child. Some may consider acquiring another handicapped child through adoption or foster-parenting. Although time and silence need to be filled, parents are encouraged to wait a year or two following the death of a child before making decisions about major changes.

Because society is not supportive of grieving parents, it is even less understanding of bereaved parents of handicapped children. Well-meaning friends and relatives often assure parents that both they and the child are now better off. This kind of response promotes parents' anger. As the mother of a Down's Syndrome child asked, "Does her disability discount her death?"

Being the parent of a disabled child and being a bereaved parent are isolating experiences. Being both is even more isolating. Because they feel a kinship, grieving parents of handicapped children seek me out. Even among bereaved parents, they fear rejection. They have had too many negative experiences in dealing with others.

Among my painful memories of Daniel is an encounter with a grocery clerk. Six-month-old Daniel sat in the shopping cart, his arms outstretched and his hands rotating rapidly. The checker stared at him, gasped, and drew herself away while exclaiming, "What's the matter with him?" When I had explained that he was merely excited, she recoiled further with a loud, "Euuh!"

Similar experiences are common among parents of handicapped children. "My children scare people," explained one parent. It is natural that the parents expect similar responses following the death of the child.

Associated guilt, anger, isolation, and emptiness make the death of a handicapped child unique. With The Compassionate Friends, however, it is the death of a child that is significant. All parents have specific circumstances and needs. The most common need is that of each other for support and understanding. As I reach out to you and you reach out to me, the differences, even the handicaps, fade in the healing and love.

"We need not walk alone. We are The Compassionate Friends."

Márcia Alig
TCF, Mercer Area, NJ

DAVID - OUR INSPIRATION

Once upon a time there was David, and that time was not so very long ago. No mother asks for a retarded child, but if you're blessed with one, you find you can't teach them so much, but they teach you. David was the youngest of my four children. He was not as pretty as my other three, but what he lacked in looks, he made up in other ways. He touched us all; everyone who knew him was touched by how hard he tried to grow up.

Not only was David retarded, he also was diagnosed at the age of ten to be suffering from a progressive deterioration of his central nervous system. He died at the age of 20, but never in all those 20 years did he give up hope for life. Just a few days before he died he said that he was thankful for being alive, even though he was already paralyzed and almost blind. His appreciation for the little he had was an example to all of us who complained when we had a great deal.

He's only a memory now of someone I used to know, but I'm a better person because of the 20 years we had together. I wouldn't have missed being his "Mama" for the world. He used to say that anything was better than nothing, and that's how I feel now that he's gone. I am making progress though, for today I was able to throw his toothbrush away.

Julia Maddox
TCF, Atlanta, GA

A SPECIAL GIFT

Once in a great while our God and Heavenly Father
chooses, in His infinite mercy and love,
to loan us a special gift.

God gave to us for a short time a flower -
a beautiful flower. Though the stem was not
perfect, the petals were.

This flower, this delicate flower, brought joy
and happiness to all who knew it. To some
it brought new experiences - a sense of compassion,
of sensitivity, of purpose. This flower created a
common bond of togetherness, of accomplishing God's
work and call as one.

The flower radiated sunshine on cloudy days, brought
a quietness in storms, a peace in turmoil.

The flower loved and was loved.

Then one day the flower began to fade and God
chose to take it home to be in His garden -
that He might enjoy its presence as we had.

And I think, now, heaven is a little brighter,
a little more beautiful.

And I know the flower is perfect in stem
as well as petals.

But we should give God thanks and praise
that He chose to share the flower with us
for a short time . . .

For Cheryl Ann Dailey
who died of multiple birth defects
by Mark Dailey
TCF, Atlanta, GA

CHAPTER VII

THERE ARE WAYS TO HELP AND HURT YOUR RECOVERY

FOUR A.M.

And does the bitter grief
Keep you awake —
Look at it full
As you would look
Into an avalanche
Sweeping your life away —
Look at that bitter grief
With conscious eyes,
As you have looked on death.
And tell your brooding sorrow
Yes, you know — that death demands
Unwavering attention.
Do not avoid that truth
Your mind repeats, repeats. —
And then there comes a truth
Beyond the truth . . .
(No, do not turn away)
Into your bitterness love finds a way
To give you comfort.

And yes, your heart will hear
The sun when night has ended.

Sascha

LEARN TO HAVE PATIENCE

TO ALL BEREAVED PARENTS:

I am a recovering bereaved parent. I was a parent by choice. One of my children died; I became a bereaved parent, certainly not by choice. As I tried to recapture the security of what was, after many agonizing months, I finally realized that I would never be the same again, that I would always hurt and miss my dead son, and that, ultimately, only I could be responsible for recovering from this hateful disease called grief.

I had to make the choice of being a bereaved parent or a recovering bereaved parent. I chose the latter. I sometimes fall off the wagon, and I know that I always will. The love of my chld will never leave me, but thank God for being a recovering bereaved parent.

It does take time, however, so don't give up on yourself. It may take more or less time for some than others. Be patient.

Eunice Guy
TCF, Atlanta, GA

BELIEVE

Believe.
Crocuses poke their heads through the
crusty snow
To let us know the long, bleak winter is
ending and
Spring will come again.

So, too, the long, bleak winter of your
Aching, breaking heart will end and
Spring will come again one day.

Be patient—but believe it—
Your spring will come again.

Betty Stevens
TCF, Baltimore, MD

SLICE OF LIFE

The scene is a very familiar one: the baby's crying, kids fighting, dog barking, doorbell ringing. The mother throws her hands over her head and pleads, "Take me away!"

This vignette meets most mothers right at gut level; how well they know the frustration the mother portrays. But for the bereaved parent this "slice of life" type of television ad evokes a different kind of reaction. Compared to grief, the irritants of daily life are mere trivialities. The bereaved parent may wish to rebuke the woman in the T.V. ad by pointing out to her that the chaos she wishes to flee is a testimonial to life. Her family is intact; she should embrace them rather than fleeing.

When days are filled with grief and pain, it is difficult to be patient with a neighbor who wails about lost sneakers, a burnt roast, chewing gum in the baby's hair, a visiting mother-in-law, and a lowered chemistry grade. It is nearly impossible to share the upset of a mere tonsillectomy when your child lies dead. The anguish of a dateless prom or a college admissions rejection dims to nonsignificance in the darkness of grief.

Patience is necessary, dear bereaved parent. Slices of life are everywhere. And because these minor frustations are the stuff that life is made of, sooner or later they will attack you as well. Although now you wish to shut off all the tiny happenings and be alone with your grief, eventually you will have to let the daily calamities in. Because you must choose life in order to go on.

One day when the car won't start because your son siphoned all the gas for his go-cart and your daughter is howling with a two-inch gash in her head from tripping over the dog who insists on sleeping on the next-to-the-top step and your husband has just called to say he won't be home from work because he's flying to Hawaii for an emergency three-day conference, you may be tempted to throw your hands over your head and plead, "Take me away!"

With patience perhaps you will pause to remember that is what you really wanted during the dark days of grief: life—in big, juicy slices.

Marcia Alig
TCF, Heightstown, NJ

DON'T LIVE IN THE PAST

"Don't live in the past." How many times have I caught myself doing just that? The past is, in a way, safe. Both my sons are alive, waiting there for that past to be played back in my mind with all the grand memories that live there. The trouble with this past is that sooner or later I must leave this safe and seemingly happy place in my mind and come again to the present. Here only one of my sons still lives. The other died two and a half years ago. Here the memories, although of happy times, bring tears to my eyes and an ache to my heart.

Crossing your bridge before you get to it is the opposite of living in the past. I often do try to cross the bridge ahead of time. How often I have said, "I wish these holidays were over; then I'd feel better," or "When the warm weather comes, I'll be happier." The truth is I'll be just a little older when the next "when" gets here, no happier, no better, just a bit older.

The fact is, the past is past - done, over. I can't be there for the good parts and I can't change the bad. As for the future, it's not here yet. That just leaves now, right now. I must learn to live now. Enjoy today and all it has to offer. Wrestle with today's problems and leave tomorrow's good and bad to be handled when tomorrow becomes today.

Sue Pierce
TCF, Bangor, ME

LEARN TO BE ASSERTIVE ABOUT YOUR RIGHT TO GRIEVE

THOUGHTS ABOUT PROGRESS

One thing that is frequently discussed at our meetings is the despair of thinking you are on the road to "recovery," when all of a sudden you seem to be back at square one. But are you really?

Let's keep in mind most of us have had no previous experience in "recovering" from the loss of a child. Therefore, we have no point of reference - it's all new to us. Actually the "roller coaster" of emotions is perfectly normal. In the very beginning most of us seem to vacillate between dead numbness and excruciating pain. Constant crying, to not a tear left - just dried up and limp. We actually are living minute to minute.

After a couple of months we might actually have a few hours that we have not cried or felt that deep overwhelming despair. Then - wham - back to where we started. We tend to panic and think something is wrong with us. Let's be realistic! There is something wrong - terribly wrong- we have each lost a child.

Let's be fair to ourselves. We started to play a role to the outside world. Like the old song says, "laughing on the outside - crying on the inside." We want to be acceptable to society. "You are doing so well," we hear. If only they knew! We may feel we have to fool others, but let us be really honest with our feelings. To deny our feelings, particularly to ourselves, is to block the road to recovery. Remember that recovery in this case does not mean "getting over it"; it means to gain control of our lives again.

So, let's not worry about what other people think, say, or expect. Our friends (well-meaning as they are), sometimes members of our family, even someone who has lost a child, should not sit in judgment. Each person grieves differently due to a person's general make-up and the relationship with the dead child. Unless someone has totally withdrawn from everything and everybody over a lengthy period of time, the chances are all is in the realm of normalcy. Only after we have walked down the long road of grief and can look back, remembering those early days and weeks, can we see we really are not on square one again. We have just slipped backwards for a time. That is all. Allow yourself that, and then strive forward again. It takes time, a lot of time! We tend to expect too much from others, others expect too much from us, and therefore we tend to expect too much from ourselves.

Mary Ehmann
TCF, Valley Forge, PA

SHOULD

I will not SHOULD on myself today. I won't let others SHOULD on me today either. Immediately after my daughter, Julie, died I was bombarded with lots of SHOULD.

You SHOULD keep a stiff upper lip, be strong for the rest of the family.

You SHOULD not dwell on it.

You SHOULD accept it as God's will. He knows best.

You SHOULD not cry about it.

Julie left a 22-month-old daughter. You SHOULD live for Autumn.

You have three other children. You SHOULD live for them.

You SHOULD not keep her paintings and photographs out in plain sight as a constant reminder.

Above all, you SHOULD keep busy. If you kept busy as I do, you wouldn't have time to think about it.

You SHOULD work in the yard, work in the house, but keep busy.

You SHOULD go back to work. You SHOULD keep so busy you won't have time to think about it.

It was fate. It was supposed to happen. You SHOULD think about all the people killed in wars, earthquakes, tornadoes, floods, airplane crashes, and all kinds of natural disasters.

You SHOULD think about Rose Kennedy, who has lost three sons, and Anne Lindberg whose baby son was kidnapped and murdered. They have survived.

You SHOULD not say such things, you SHOULD not even think them.

One of my best friends now is a "new" friend. She came by the office one day and invited me to go for a cup of coffee. Immediately after being seated she said, "Jean, I don't know how you feel. I don't know what you are going through. I haven't experienced it. If you'd like to tell me how you feel or talk about Julie, please do." I can tell her anything. She is never shocked. She never says any SHOULD to me. I value her friendship.

I feel many people have awarded themselves Doctorates of SHOULD. One woman is particularly full of SHOULD. If I ever catch her mouth shut long enough, I'd really like to apply a generous amount of a good brand of super glue. This Dr. of SHOULD knows exactly how I SHOULD feel and exactly what I SHOULD do to get better. But this same Dr. of SHOULD, upon hearing one of her children or grandchildren has or is planning some triviality she doesn't agree with, is so upset she's flat on her back in bed (and on occasion has had to hospitalized over it). Of course, I'd like to do something about this sort of person, but it's probably illegal or at least unseemly. However, it SHOULD be perfectly permissible to put a bug down her blouse or a mouse up her pant leg.

I'm sure you've all had this problem. You've heard the same or similar SHOULDS. Most of my experience has been with "her," but I'm sure bereaved fathers have had a lot of SHOULD from "him" too. Have you noticed that all this SHOULD comes from people whose children are living?

Just for today, don't let anybody SHOULD on you.

Jean Corley Lacy,
TCF, Lindsey, OK

ALLOWING GRIEF IN OUR SOCIETY

One of the biggest problems I had with my grief was in allowing myself to grieve. I was caught up in the societal expectations I had grown up with: "Don't cry," "Be brave," "Keep a stiff upper lip." When I look back I can see how harmful that was. I was filled with "shoulds" and "should nots," "oughts," and ought nots." I never stopped and asked myself WHY I should not or ought not. If I had, I would have realized that I was only doing what society expected me to do. Society was telling me to do what was necessary to make it comfortable. Society couldn't handle my negative emotions. Society, for me, was my friends and relatives. I could laugh and be happy with them, but I dared not cry or show unhappiness with them. If I did, I made them uncomfortable, and I wasn't to do that.

My soul cried out for release of my emotions. I wanted to cry and scream and lash out at the world in my anger. I wanted to confess my guilts. I wanted to tell someone I hurt so terribly. I wanted to talk and talk and talk about Arthur. But I could not, I should not, I ought not. I was a victim of not only the most devastating thing that can happen to a person—his child's death—but also of a society that denied death and the emotions that resulted from the loss of the most important parts of one's life.

Those were society's expectations in 1971. They are not much different today. There are some small breakthroughs being made in respect to how society looks at death, dying and grief by Elisabeth Kubler-Ross and others, and groups such as Make Today Count, SIDS, and, of course, The Compassionate Friends. But society is far from accepting death and grief as inevitable and the pain of the survivors as real, needing expression. Society is far from allowing negative emotions, much less allowing our sharing of our pain with them. We can change that.

With every great change that society has made there had to be a beginning. There had to be small changes in people, and ideas grew until many people changed. So it is up to us, each in his own way, to work toward changing society's expectations for the grieving person. We can begin with our own family and friends. We must tell them of our needs in our grief and ask them to help us.

This will not be easy at first. We, too, are part of that death-denying society. We, too, have in the past been uncomfortable with another's negative emotions, but we must try. Specifically, we must tell our relatives and friends that we need to talk about our child and our grief. At the same time, we must tell them we know it is uncomfortable for them. Honesty and openness are necessary. We must be patient with them. We are going to find friends or relatives who refuse to listen or to allow us to discuss our feelings and emotions. Some will be completely unable to help us. Their own life experiences will not allow them to get close to our pain as we are asking them to do. With these people we must try not to be critical and think they are unfeeling or do not care. With gentle persistence we will at least have let them know how they can help us. Whether they help us or not must be their choice.

Our childrens' deaths have made us painfully aware of the needs of bereaved parents. It has also made us aware that there is little knowledge in our society of these needs. Each of us can do something to raise this awareness in others. Hopefully, ten or twenty years from now society will look at the grieving person and say: "It's okay to cry," "Tell me about your loved one," "I'll listen to your angers, your guilts, and your fears and not judge," and we will be able to say that we were a part of that change.

Margaret Gerner
TCF, St. Louis, MO

DO IT YOUR WAY

I think it's only fair to tell you - there is no bereaved parent of the month award, nor an award for the one with the stiffest upper lip! In fact, what you will find if you try to be the most stoic, brave and strong, the one doing too well, is instead of a reward, you suffer the consequences.

It is not possible to lose someone as vital as one's child and not have the pain of deep grief. You will find a great many non-bereaved people will encourage you to play the old game of, "if you'll pretend you're okay and it's not really so bad, we'll let you come play with us, but if you're going to cry and talk about your dead child, then you can't play."

This is one time in your life you don't have to meet anybody else's standards. There is nothing more unique about you than the way you express your grief - and you have that right, however it is manifested. A great deal of how you go about it is determined by how you have handled previous losses.

So, if someone tries to influence you to play the old game by rewarding you with attention because "you're doing so well," tell them you're not doing well. Tell them your child has died and you're hurting. Let them know it doesn't help you for them to pretend everything is okay. Do whatever it is you need to do to survive this trauma and don't worry about whether it pleases of displeases other people. . . . DO IT YOUR WAY!!

Mary Cleckley
TCF, Atlanta, GA

LEARN TO FORGIVE

FORGIVE UNTIL FOREVER

Grieving is a fierce and overwhelming expression of love thrust upon us by a deep and hurtful loss. Yet grieving is frequently such an entanglement of feelings we often fail to recognize that ultimately forgiveness must be an integral part of our grief and our healing. For what is love if forgiveness is silent within us?

We learn to forgive our children for dying, ourselves for not preventing it. We begin to forgive our God or the fate we see ruling our universe. We start to forgive relatives and friends for abandoning us in their own bewilderment over the onslaught of emotions they sense in our words and behavior.

I believe we must be open to the balm of forgiveness. Through its expression in our lives, be it through thought, word or deed, we find small ways to seek life once more. Deep within us, forgiveness is capable of treading the wasteland of our souls to help us feel again the love that has not died.

It is the beginning of release from the dominance of pain, not from the continual hurt of missing those we have lost, but from lacking the fullness of the love we shared with our child. That love lives with strength inside ourselves and yet our beings are so entrapped in a whirling vortex of anger, despair, frustration, abandonment and depression that we often feel it only lightly.

Let us all heed the quiet message heard so softly in that maelstrom of the spirit. Forgive, forgive, and forgive until forever. Let love enfold our anguish, helping us to learn to grow and strive beyond this hour to a rich tomorrow.

Don Hackett
TCF, South Shore Chapter, MA

SPRING CLEANING

I am a "spring cleaner." As one who works full time, my usual housecleaning is what is often called "a lick and a promise." But once a year I really enjoy taking everything out of a closet, bureau, cabinet or cupboard - examining it - remembering (if I can) where it came from - thinking about its potential uses - and often wondering why I am keeping it!

Recently, as I was rummaging around on a shelf, finding a few things I'd forgotten about, I thought about how much of what I was doing could apply to my "personal closet," as well as to our living room closet. My "personal closet" is that part of me where I store all sorts of things - anger, guilt, hope, joy, love, caring. If I could dig way down into that closet and find something I'd forgotten I had and could put to good use, I'd like to find a big box labeled "FORGIVENESS."

One of the things we must do before we can move ahead in any situation is to completely forgive whatever wrongs, real or imagined (and we do have both), have been done to us. This isn't easy.

I have to forgive the doctors and nurses. Their training had not prepared them to deal with a child whose illness they couldn't understand or to be supportive of her grieving parents and sister.

I have to forgive the people who stayed away from us because they had never been taught about the needs of bereaved parents.

I have to forgive the people who tried to "cheer us up" or "take our minds off it." They, too, were baffled by the horror of it all and were, in their own way, trying to be helpful.

I have to forgive the people who told us that Linda's death was God's will. They were trying to comfort us.

I have to forgive myself - for so many things. This is a really tough one - the times I was cross or demanding, the situations I handled badly as Linda was growing up, the times I screamed or spanked out of my own frustration. I think she has forgiven me, yet the guilt remains, and I must forgive myself.

Then there are the questions so many of us ask, "Why didn't I realize sooner how sick she was?" "Why didn't we transfer her to Children's Hospital sooner?" There are no answers to these questions. If I made mistakes, then I must accept them and forgive myself for them. I know that carrying the burden of blaming myself and passing judgment on myself will only weigh me down and hold back whatever potential I have for future growth. But still it's difficult.

I have to forgive people who don't understand where I'm coming from now and make derogatory remarks about their children. I do wish I could help them to appreciate how very valuable and precious those little lives are.

And, finally, I have to forgive Linda. Her dying really messed up my life by creating a situation I didn't know how to deal with. It took a relatively normal, uncomplicated life, smashed it to smithereens, and forced me to attempt to reconstruct it - to put it back together - a hard job when some of the pieces don't quite fit anymore!

Yes, I'd like to find deep down inside me a great big box labeled "FORGIVENESS."

Evelyn Billings
TCF, Springfield, MA

FORGIVENESS . . .

When our child dies, most of us are angry at those who caused or had a part in the death. Sometimes we are angry at our child for leaving us this way. We did not deserve the hurt and now it is lodged deep in our memory.

As we attend Compassionate Friends meetings, we can see we are not alone in this hurting. It gives us the chance to share and try to understand the pain.

Sometimes some of us even hate, although we don't want to admit that hate. I think if we admit the hate, talk about it, bring it up in group meetings, then we can resolve it and slowly turn these feelings into forgiveness.

I feel that we must separate the thing we are angry about from the persons. In my case, I was angry at the doctors in the emergency room who I felt let my daughter die. Then I began to see that doctors do not JUST LET a sixteen-year-old die. Then I knew it was the death and not the doctors with whom I was angry. I guess they were just the scapegoats.

A lot of us are angry at God for taking our child, but then what kind of God would take such a beautiful person. Not the God I know. He would never hurt us or our child.

Forgiveness is hard, but we must persist. We must not think we are letting the person we are angry with off the hook. Someone even told me forgiveness is a sign of weakness and I should be strong and not forgive. I believe vengeance does not even the score. I believe it just makes our anger deeper. We don't forgive and we just go in a vicious circle.

Let us work on forgiving. We can survive on love, but not on hate. Let us love the child we lost, love his memory. When we turn from anger to love, the forgiveness will begin.

We must forgive us, as some of us are angry at ourselves. Forgiveness for some of us will be hard to reach. Keep working on it, keep loving. We cannot control the future, but we can be a part in the successful outcome.

Larry Warren
TCF, North Georgia Chapter

ACCEPTANCE

In Robert Redford's latest movie, "The Natural," there is a line that really touched me because I could relate to it so well. Redford plays a talented baseball player who has always dreamed of being the best baseball player the world has ever seen. Although he is a dynamic player, certain events in his life prevent him from realizing his dream while he is young. Many years later he tells his girlfriend how frustrated and angry he feels about nothing in his life turning out as he planned. She nods her head gently to show she understands, and then she says softly, "I think each of us really has two lives to live - one that we learn with and one that we live with."

It would be wonderful if every baby born into this world came with a warranty: "This child guaranteed to be free from defect in workmanship for 75 years or your money cheerfully refunded." But life doesn't come with any guarantees, especially when it relates to children. We live in an imperfect world and as long as there are diseases, accidents, and human failure, we must learn to live with the unexpected. Now, quite honestly, I don't really like the fact that I can't control the destiny of my children. Other than fulfilling their physical needs to the best of my ability and trying to instill in them honest, loving values, there are simply some things over which I am powerless. And that makes me frustrated. Like Robert Redford, I, too, have witnessed the death of a dream.

I had so many plans for my little girl. I wanted her to take piano lessons and learn ballet and enjoy art. (Of course, it is conceivable that she would have preferred to play football instead, and I'm sure that with a little effort I could have accepted that!) But I never had a chance to realize that dream with her. Every bereaved parent can relate to what I am saying. You can understand how devastating it is to be robbed of all of the loving potential your child represents. This is life's deepest heartache, I believe, for although we expected to someday lose our grandparents, our parents, or even our spouse, none of us really thought we would have to give up our child. And, like Redford, we are now faced with the realization that so many of the things we had hoped for simply haven't materialized.

Where do we go from here? Is there a key to help us unlock part of the mystery of how to cope after the death of a child? I believe so, although it's not easy. But I believe it's the only way to bring about lasting inner peace and healing. It is acceptance.

Please don't misunderstand me. I am not suggesting that we should deny all emotion, for it would be impossible to escape the anger, sadness, guilt, and depression that is a normal part of the grieving process. Nor am I in favor of repressing our need to ask "Why?" I do not believe we should unquestioningly resign ourselves to our child's death. There is nothing wrong with wanting a reason for this tragedy. In fact, it is this realization of the injustice of it all which keeps us inspired to find a cure for cancer and other diseases and which gives us the stamina to change the laws to get drunk drivers off of our highways. But even though there is nothing wrong with searching for answers, we must also realize that we will probably never find all of the answers.

There are simply some mysteries about life and death that no man can understand, and to refuse to accept this will only lead to more turmoil and bitterness. We can curse this reality, we can deny it, or we can cry over it, but sooner or later we must accept it. No one but God can tell us why our children died. We may try to blame circumstances, doctors, or even ourselves, but ultimately we must accept the fact that there are many unanswered questions. And we must go on with life as well as we possibly can, taking what we have learned in this experience and sharing that knowledge with others going through the same heartache.

Yes, each of us does have two lives, "one that we learn with and one that we live with." The death of a child will certainly change us, but it does not have to destroy us. Clinging to the bitterness and anger will only prolong our misery; it does not bring our child back to us or help us cope with this tragedy. Acceptance enables us to take the broken, scattered pieces of the puzzle of our lives, and slowly, one by one, start putting them back together again. The picture may not look just like we had hoped it would; there may even be a few lost pieces that we can never find again. But the final result can still be beautiful and meaningful, a life full of inspiration for those who have the pleasure of sharing it.

Diane Roddam
TCF, El Paso, TX

ACCEPTING THE UNACCEPTABLE

What a paradox - accepting the unacceptable! And how very much the very idea grates against those of us who have lost children to death. We detest the explanations offered by well-meaning friends. They cannot begin to understand how unacceptable is our loss! I write knowing this, but asking that we look at this idea of accepting the unacceptable and see just what it may mean to us, and how we may, in time, do that very thing - accept the unacceptable. I believe that this acceptance must take place if healing from our grief is to occur.

An oft quoted prayer reads, "God grant me the serenity to accept the things I cannot change, courage to change the things I can, and the wisdom to know the difference." Most of us have had our faiths, no matter how different they may be, severely tested by the deaths of our children. In my case all the anger I have been able to muster has been expressed with a raised fist to God, accompanied by the question "Why?" This "Why?" is what makes it seem so impossible for us to accept the deaths of our children. Acceptance is not an explanation. So let us not confuse the need for acceptance of the tragedy we have experienced and our felt need for understanding it. They are not the same.

When all of us first suffered bereavement, protective shock and numbness gave many of us the semblance that we were accepting the tragedy very well. Some of our friends commented on how well we were doing. We may have even felt so ourselves. Remember? That was a form of acceptance which arose because we did not know what else to do. We had more immediate needs to be met, the need of making the arrangements for the funeral and the needs of our families. The need to begin picking up the pieces and returning to work or school or our other daily tasks provided us with some acceptance of what had happened. And yet, how many times did we have that strong feeling that this was really just a dream and we would awake and find it was not so? How many times did we see the loved one in the store or someplace and then, at least temporarily, think that the drean was over and all was now well again? After some time, different for each of us, reality began to sink in. The strong wish to deny the death came upon us with a heaviness that seemed unbearable, accompanied by extreme anger and guilt all mixed up together. Our thoughts included that things would never be the same again. We also felt that we would never "get back to normal" as we were urged to by our friends. We were correct, for we never will return to the old normal. But these facts do not mean that we cannot achieve acceptance.

In acceptance, we can choose to think of the happy times we had with our children, for there were many. We now can elect to recall these precious memories. We can learn to laugh in recalling humorous events from the past. We could not control the events that led to the death of our children, nor can we control the sad memories that return unexpectedly. But we can choose to recall the many pleasant times, and express our gratitude for them. In accepting the unacceptable, we have not forgotten the unforgettable, we do not understand that which is not understandable. We still love and miss our children very much. They cannot return that love openly to us as they did in the past. But they do return that love in our memories.

The refusal to accept what is unacceptable only prolongs our anger and guilt, and produces bitterness. It does not relieve that deep aching which seems as if it will never lessen. But the mind set which brings acceptance is accompanied by the requested serenity. The serenity and acceptance bring with them the courage to proceed with the changes which must now exist in our new "normal." With serenity, acceptance, courage and change comes a wisdom, the realization that some things which were so important before, no longer are as important. And some things which didn't seem to matter as much before, now have assumed a greater importance in our lives. Our tragedies did not come so that we might learn these things, but acceptance of that which we could not prevent has allowed us to learn and mature.

Chaplain Lorna Kuyk spoke recently to bereaved parents at an interfaith service. She referred to young Hebrew men in captivity in a strange land. These young men were asked to sing their captors some of their old songs. We bereaved parents ask with them, "How can we sing the songs of old?" for we too are captives in a foreign land, not of our choosing. Chaplain Kuyk advised us that we must learn to sing new songs in a strange land. We cannot return to the former days and former ways. But out of our experiences can come new songs, springing from the heart. These will be ours only as we achieve acceptance of the unacceptable.

Excerpts from an article
by Robert F. Gloor
TCF, Tuscaloosa, AL

LETTING GO

SHARING

One evening at the kitchen table my four-year-old daughter, Barbara, watched with interest as I was preparing to mail out some letters concerning The Compassionate Friends. She showed a keen interest in the logo sticker I attached to the corner of a large brown envelope. Her big blue eyes took on a seriousness I had never seen before as she asked, "Mom, why is the 'kid' so far away from the hands?"

I replied as honestly as I could, "Because the 'kid' has died and the hands are a mommy's or daddy's reaching for their child."

She turned those blue eyes to meet mine and said, "I think you're wrong, Mom. I think the hands are letting him go."

How remarkably perceptive children are! I sat there astonished by what she had suggested; then I grabbed a pen to write down what she had said. This was, I thought, a sage piece of wisdom from someone who believes in Santa, the Tooth Fairy and wishing on stars. Barbara, in her innocent way, made me see that I am still reaching. It has been two years since B. J. was stillborn, but I continue to reach for something. Just what that something is I don't know, but I'll know what it is when I find it. Perhaps then a part of me can let go. Do children sense that death is a process of "letting go;" that letting go is okay for those whose time it is to "let go?" I don't have an answer but maybe my blue-eyed, blonde-haired Barbara does. Maybe, just maybe, all children do . . .

Edith Fraser
TCF, Winnipeg, Canada

PRACTICING THE ART OF LETTING GO

Ten years of experiencing the loss of my son Daniel and six years working with other bereaved parents have taught me that letting go is not a one-time act but a process which overlaps the grief process and which requires practice and work. However, it is something familiar to all of us, for we have been practicing letting go since we first recognized fairy tales as fancy rather than truth. It is also not necessary for a bereaved person to wait until a certain point of grief before letting go. Rather, the grieving person may start letting go as grief begins.

Many of us have assisted our children in letting go as we helped them adjust to nursery school, celebrated a lost tooth, or watched them nail a "Private - Keep out" sign on the door of their room. We are, therefore, all experienced at letting go and need not think of it as a frightening or negative undertaking. Rather, most of our previous experiences with it have been as positive as growing up or helping our children mature. Therefore, we should not resist trying it as a part of the grief process.

There are many methods of letting go. Conscious decision, notes to your child, prayer, family meeting, or symbolic acts are some successful ones. For a first attempt you could try using note paper and a helium balloon (easily found in shopping malls or grocery stores). On the paper write what it is that you wish to let go. This could be a nagging guilt, something left unsaid or not taken back, an unfulfilled wish, a regret, a specific anger, etc. It could also be a task pertaining to the child's death such as sorting personal items or clothing, rearranging the child's room, ordering a monument, providing for a memorial, or cancelling appointments and subscriptions. The note could be written after the task was completed or as a commitment to accomplish it. After you have written what you wish to let go, attach the note to the string of the helium balloon, walk outside and release the balloon. As you watch the balloon rise, feel the weight of what you had placed on the balloon lift away from you. Watch it until it fades from view, enjoying the feeling of lightness as it disappears.

Do not expect its release to change your life completely, but in the next several weeks try letting go of other aspects of your grief. The anger at your friends who fail to call, the hurt of the thoughtless who wish you "Happy Mothers's or Father's Day," the sudden rush of tears when you hear your child's favorite song can all be let go one at a time.

It's not easy. I know. It is ten years after Daniel's death and I am still discovering how much I have lost. And I am still letting go.

Marcia Alig
TCF, Mercer Chapter, NJ
Excerpts from an article which appeared
in the fall 1985 National TCF Newsletter

LITTLE BY LITTLE

I once thought that my only link to you
was my grief.
I couldn't let go.
I knew if I did
I would lose us both.

But, one day
when I couldn't take the pain anymore,
I decided to try.
So, slowly and carefully
I let go of my deathline to you,
and I was surprised to find myself
being held by God.

Little by little, step by step,
I learned that I didn't need
to hang on to the death
to remember the life.
What a joyous discovery!

Kittie Brown McGowin
TCF, Montgomery, AL

ARE YOU STUCK IN YOUR GRIEF?

It is a few years down the road and life still has no meaning? You're still severely depressed. You heard "it" gets better with time but you keep asking when? Meetings were supposed to help so you've been going only to find they too have not provided the answer? Could it be you are stuck in your grief and don't want to feel any differently than you do?

A bereaved mother called just recently and said what surprised her since her teenage daughter was killed in an auto accident was how relatives clearly had not learned anything from her daughter's death. It didn't help them appreciate what they have—their own families, their health, having food on their tables. They had not learned. Have we, the parents of the children whose deaths brought us to TCF? Have we learned that it's what we have left that counts?

In my role as co-chapter leader of our chapter, I have talked to many bereaved parents, siblings and relatives over the last four and a half years since my eight-year-old daughter, Cassandra, died of a brain stem tumor. Some bereaved parents refuse to accept a helping hand. They are negative and any attempt to gently help them along is rebuffed. They wear their bereaved parenthood as a rationale to express their rage toward everyone around them - their spouses, their surviving families, their coworkers, restaurant personnel, even merchants when they are out shopping.

We each bring into our grief our own strengths and weaknesses but this does not excuse our being stuck. Grief is hard work; however, we can choose not to work at it. We can spend our remaining years complaining to the world around us and seek out others who do likewise or use our loss as a tool by which to grow.

If you think that you felt "better" last year or the year before, perhaps you have stopped working at your grief. To feel life is less painful you need to realize that grief is an ongoing job.

If your phone rings less often, could it be that even your friends at TCF are finding that you never have anything positive to say, so to protect themselves they, too, stay away?

Is it that meetings are not helpful to you or that you won't let them be a source of help? Is it that time doesn't heal or you refuse to use the time constructively?

Consider accepting a helping hand. You might be pleasantly surprised. Or better yet, offer to help someone else. It could help you to focus your energy away from yourself and you might find you, too, can be a source of strength to others. It could give you the incentive to no longer be stuck.

Does being less unhappy really mean a betrayal of our children? Surely we know we will never be the same. However, being stuck does not mean we have forgotten our children. Our love lives on. What can each of us do in memory of our children that will also help us?

Angela Purpura
TCF, Long Island, NY Chapter

IT SEEMS TO ME . . .

"Letting Go" is a peculiar proposition. It's been talked about a lot. But sometimes, on reflection, or at the moment—the explanations don't seem to make sense.

After pondering, I think—perhaps—"letting go" means:

—being willing to stop being miserable
—being willing to relax, and go with the flow of everyday living
—being willing to enjoy life's pleasures, small or large.

"Letting go" does not mean forgetting our child. It means putting aside the dank, gloomy, gray abomination that is early grieving. It does take time to pick from our faces the strands of the wet dirty mop and from our shoulders the ton of cement that are our early burden.

One life has stopped. Living goes on. So should we, knowing that loving need never end.

Joan D. Schmidt
TCF, Central Jersey, NJ

TAKE CARE OF YOUR HEALTH

MANAGING STRESS WHILE GRIEVING

Early On:

1. Make no final decisions now about anything.
2. Ask for help in guidance through daily patterns such as child care, meal preparation, phone calls, etc.
3. Feel whatever comes - don't be afraid of your feelings. Talk about your child and what has happened whenever you can.
4. Force yourself to eat properly if you have lost your appetite. Take a vitamin (stress) supplement.
5. Move your body - exercise. Walking is the best and easiest.
6. Sleep more - when you want to. If you can't sleep, tire yourself with exercise. At least rest.
7. If you can - pray.

Later On:

1. Simplify your life for the time being. Do only what must be done. Be structured and predictable.
2. Eat properly.
3. Exercise fairly vigorously and often.
4. Plan times to talk about your child and your experiences. Be intentional about it.
5. Forgive yourself over and over again - for the past, for your feelings, for anything, real or imaginary.
6. Allow your family to grieve or seek help in their own way. Be sympathetic but do not try to solve their grief or seek help from them at this time.
7. Be honest - let people know how you are. Yet don't succumb to the need to dump. Don't let anyone push you to "getting over it" before you can. At the same time, it is not the fault of your friends that they do not know what to say or do.
8. Continue to love your family and significant friends and find small ways to show it.
9. Survive.

Still Later:

1. *Establish new rituals in your family around holidays and special occasions, even around daily patterns.*
2. *Force yourself, at the moments when you feel you are getting close to acceptance, to let yourself laugh or rest or forget for a moment. You don't need a forever pain in order to remember or love your child.*
3. *Find a project, a cause, a charity, a task to which you can devote your energy and frustrated love; this can be a way to make the life and death of your child have some personal meaning for you.*
4. *Love your family and yourself.*
5. *If you will, continue to pray — for strength and comfort.*

Six Things Necessary For Managing Stress

1. *Balanced nutrition*
2. *Keep your fluid intake high*
3. *Avoid caffeine, alcohol, sugar in excess*
4. *Exercise*
5. *Get adequate rest*
6. *Use your social network for support*

Florence Miller
TCF, Columbia, SC

ESCAPE?

It is not the intent of The Compassionate Friends to impose rules upon you, nor do we assume the right to determine your moral values or life styles. What we do try to do is point out potential problem areas during the most painful part of your grief so that you can, hopefully, recognize and avoid some of these pitfalls.

When a child dies, the pain of the loss is so deep and ever present that the people who are grieving for the child sometimes seek ways to escape that pain. If you have been to our meetings, read our newsletter, or talked to our telephone friends, you know that we encourage you to face the fact that there is no real way for you to escape permanently from the pain of losing a child. You loved; therefore, you grieve. You may succeed in postponing your grief for a time, but it will resurface some day in some way. You are encouraged to deal with it now so that it won't be waiting ten or fifteen years down the road for you.

One of the most obvious ways for some to attempt to postpone or escape the pain is to turn to drugs, such as excessive amounts of alcohol, tranquilizers, mood elevators, and sleeping pills. You may even find that your physician will prescribe some of these things for you in an effort to make you "better." We do not speak, of course, about those who have medical or emotional problems that are separate and apart from the normal pain of grief. We speak, instead, of the process that normally follows the death of a child, and in this instance, these drugs do not cure or make you better; they simply postpone the grief process. They may even make it worse. Alcohol, for instance, is a depressant, as are tranquilizers for some people. What can happen then is you go from the normal depression of grief to an even more depressed state. The mood elevators give you the false impression that you have things under control. When you finish with all of these things, guess what is waiting for you? Your unresolved grief, and it may then be complicated by a drug dependency or disguised as mental or physical ailments.

I am simply suggesting here that you recognize that grief is normal and necessary when you have lost something or somebody important to you. The pain, depression, hopelessness, inability to sleep, frustration, anger, guilt, loss of your goals and aims, loss of the ability to maintain an organized pattern in your life, and confusion are all a part of the symptoms of grief. You can't have softening of these symptoms until you have allowed yourself to feel whatever is necessary and normal for you under these circumstances. When you do allow yourself to hurt and feel these things, it hastens the day when you can emerge on the other side of of the most painful part of grief, having survived in an emotionally healthy way. There are no shortcuts, only postponements, and you will do yourself and your doctor a favor if you resist asking for prescriptions to relieve these normal symptoms.

The hurt you are feeling is a sign that you are dealing with your grief, and that means you are making progress. It takes time and patience. If you have already tried to escape and found that it doesn't work, please seek help from organizations that work with drug dependencies.

IT WILL BE BETTER! But you have to hurt before you reach that place. Truly this is a time when the kindest thing you can do for yourself is allow yourself to feel the normal symptoms of grief. Running and hiding doesn't work, but patience does.

Mary Cleckley
TCF, Atlanta, GA

MAKING IT THROUGH THE FIRST YEAR

Don't Be Afraid Of Your Feelings and Don't Run Away From Them: Let yourself feel them. Cry, be angry, express your feelings. You may experience intense pain, feelings of unreality, isolation, exhaustion, panic, fear, reality distortion, deep depression, loneliness, emptiness, anger and guilt. You are not going crazy (which is something everyone worries about). Grief is extremely painful, but it is the cost of commitment to those we love. Grief is a process; it is hard work, but the only way to reach the other side of it is to go through it. Learn to flow with your feelings of grief, and know that, although they are painful, they are not permanent. Your sense of reality, your concentration will come back. You will function again.

Share Your Feelings: Telling the story helps. Each time it is told there may be a small feeling of relief. Eventually, although you may like to talk about your child's life, you will no longer have the compulsion to review his death.

Find A Creative Outlet: Any outlet which requires physical involvement (needlework, painting, building a patio, or other projects) can be very helpful. It may also help to reduce the feeling of powerlessness by providing a sense of control through completing a task. A little later, reading about grief can provide information and understanding. Keeping a journal of your thoughts and feelings can also be an excellent outlet, especially if you don't have someone to whom you can talk.

Turn To God: Your religious belief can be most sustaining, although there may be many things you may not understand. If you feel anger toward God, talk to him and express that anger. As you do so, you may find your anger dissipating and being replaced by the strength you need.

Take Time In Small Manageable Chunks: Although difficult to do, it is worth the the effort to take just one day at a time. Don't borrow trouble by sitting around dreading something (like Christmas or your child's birthday) which may be three months down the road. Today is all you have to worry about.

Set Goals: At first these may be exceedingly simple. But it is very important not to wait until you become interested in something before you begin to do it. Try anyway; the interest comes in doing. By setting goals and attempting to reach them, you may find that you will establish a new routine. This is important.

Utilize Support Groups: For us, The Compassionate Friends has been a fantastic help. We had been feeling totally isolated. Suddenly we were in a room full of people who had gone through the same experience, and they were still living and surviving! As the months passed we began to look forward more and more to sharing our feeling with people who actually knew what we were talking about. There seems to be an instant bonding among people who have lost children.

Don't Try To Live Up To Other People's Expectations: It's your child who is dead. It's your grief. There are no "shoulds" except for one. You "should" pretty much go with your own feelings and your own timetable. We recently attended the Regional Conference of TCF where John Claypool, author of Tracks of a Fellow Struggler, was the keynote speaker. He said "Until you have been through the entire calendar, you have not experienced the full extent of the loss. You don't sow and reap in the same day. Impatience comes from people who are dealing with this grief on a much more superficial level than you are."

Don't Turn To Medication Or Alcohol: This is extremely important. If you feel you are being given or kept on too much medication, change doctors or get a second opinion. The experience of grief is bad enough itself; you don't need it complicated by dependence on medication or alcohol. There is a certain amount of grief and pain you have to endure: medication only postpones the grieving process.

Watch Your Health: The state of your health is of the utmost importance. Without the proper food and rest, your mind won't be able to deal with the shock of the situation. It is vital to eat a balanced diet and to get the proper amount of sleep and exercise.

*Don't Expect Too Much From Your Spouse: When a tragedy happens, it is a shock to find, as Harriet Schiff says in **The Bereaved Parent,** that it is hard to lean on something that is already bent double. Learn to accept and respect each other's methods of grieving even if you don't understand. If your spouse if having a bad day, say you're sorry, that you understand, but don't try to get him to come out of his mood, or try to entertain him to get his mind off it. Communicate; you don't have to talk all the time, but please try to remember - in most cases you and your spouse had a relationship apart from your child.*

Don't Be Too Hard On Yourself: The "guilties" can be very damaging. Treat yourself as kindly and with as much respect as you would treat someone else who was going through this same experience.

Don't Prolong Your Grief To Keep Yourself Close To Your Child: Maintaining a state of grief on a severe plateau is not maintaining a closeness with your child. This is a false impression. Letting go of pain does not mean letting go of your child. Don't feel guilty about feeling better.

Don't Take What People Say To You Too Seriously: You will hear all kinds of platitudes: "Hold your chin up," "Well, at least you can have other children," "Be grateful that you have each other," "I know just how you feel: I lost my 96-year-old great-aunt last year." Sometimes it will hurt, sometimes it will make you angry. Try to cultivate a sense of humor. Most people mean well, they're not out to hurt you. They just don't know what to say. Our daughter, Shannon, when asked what she would say to a person whose child had died, replied, "I would say, 'I love you'." If we all took lessons from six-year-olds, we might know what to say.

Excerpts from an article
by Judy and Jim Taylor
TCF, Birmingham, AL

WHEN IT HURTS TOO MUCH TO TALK . . . WRITE!

I never thought of a typewriter as a therapist until my son died. I still don't think of it as Dr. Smith-Corona, but there's no doubt it has played an active role in resolving my grief. Maybe it's because I don't always understand exactly how I feel until I see what I think on paper.

If some aspects of your child's death are too painful to talk about, or if you seem to be stuck at some point in your grief work, you too may find that the process of writing your thoughts out will help you clarify and come to grips with them. You can write anytime you need to talk, if you know how to make a pencil work. That is particularly useful in the dark of night when your struggles with grief seem to intensify and sleep eludes you.

Writing can be an especially important release to parents who didn't have a chance to say goodby. Write a letter detailing how much his love meant to you and expressing your regret because you didn't get to tell him that. You may want to tuck the letter away with some of your child's possessions, or burn it and scatter the ashes on his grave or where you feel the wind will carry it to him.

Writing is also a safe way to discharge anger that would otherwise be directed towards your mate. Painful words hurled at a spouse can never be reclaimed or their memory totally erased, but if they are committed to paper instead, they can be burned when your rage has subsided, or hidden and reevaluated at a later date.

An additional advantage I discovered is that writing diminished the guilt I felt over my son's death. I suspect that is frequently the case because it is so easy to list our real or imagined shortcomings when we're grieving, and so hard to remember all the good and right and special things we did to try to preserve our children's lives.

But perhaps the most compelling reason of all to write is that it preserves their memory, and that is a very special love gift to our family and our friends. The finished product doesn't have to be bound in leather. It is a priceless gift even if it is handwritten and tucked in a plastic folder.

I had been a professional writer for several years before our son, Eric, died, but after his death I found it hard to write about anything except him and the way I felt. And I couldn't do much of that at one time without soaking my paper with tears. So I began writing little pieces for our chapter newsletter. In each of those I talked about one aspect of my grief. No more. Don't try to tell your child's whole story at once, don't try to describe your grief in the space of a page. Do it bit by bit.

Start by picking up that pencil or sitting down at the keyboard and writing about one happy incident in your child's life. Don't worry about form or punctuation or spelling. Just tell about that incident from start to finish. Describe the day, the setting, the sounds, the smells, the prevailing emotions and the people involved.

One word of caution is in order here. When you are writing, it is all too easy to remember the good things your child did and forget about the ornery, naughty things that made him or her real. Those must be included if your word portrait is to be a three dimensional picture.

Do this exercise three or four times and each time you repeat it, write about a different special time including at least one story you could introduce by saying, "You won't believe what he did today."

Looking at family albums and reading old letters can help you recreate those scenes. So can playing remember-when with family members and friends who were involved and can help you fill in details you might have forgotten.

One way to begin that is to interview yourself. Pretend that you are going to write a story about a mother or father like yourself who has lost a child under circumstances almost identical to those surrounding your child's death. Make a list of questions to ask that hypothetical person and be sure to include all the ones you wish someone would give you a chance to answer.

Arrange the questions as nearly as possible into a chronological order and tackle them one at a time, answering each as completely as you can. As you work through the list, you'll remember things you wish you'd said in answering previous questions. Consequently, using a separate sheet of paper for each will make it easier for you to add to them.

I think the advantages of writing about our grief far outweigh the disadvantages. Perhaps the greatest disadvantage is the fact that this exercise is painful. It just plain hurts to mine our souls, and we have to dig deep if we are to get it all out. Despite this, or because of it, writing is a healing exercise. The work can be emotionally exhausting. When I was writing a book about my son, some chapters took so much out of me that I had to put the manuscript away for several weeks before I could face it again. However, the day it was finally finished a curtain fell on my grief. After I had said everything that I needed to say, I was physically and emotionally spent, but within a few days the curtain rose and a new me stepped forth.

That's what writing about grief does for you. Writing helps you come to grips with grief and then go on to something else.

Judy Osgood
TCF, Central Oregon Chapter
Excerpts from an article in the TCF National Newsletter

BEYOND SURVIVING

1. *Know you can survive. You may not think so, but you can.*
2. *Struggle with "why" it happened until you no longer need to know "why" or until you are satisfied with partial answers.*
3. *Know you may feel overwhelmed by the intensity of your feelings but all your feelings are normal.*
4. *Anger, guilt, confusion, forgetfulness are common responses. You are not crazy - you are in mourning.*
5. *Be aware you may feel appropriate anger at the person, at the world, at God, at yourself.*
6. *You may feel guilty for what you think you did or did not do.*
7. *Having suicidal thoughts is common. It does not mean that you will act on those thoughts.*
8. *Remember to take one moment or one day at a time.*
9. *Find a good listener with whom to share. Call someone if you need to talk.*
10. *Don't be afraid to cry. Tears are healing.*
11. *Give yourself time to heal.*
12. *Remember the choice was not yours. No one is the sole influence in another's life.*
13. *Expect setbacks. Don't panic if emotions return like a tidal wave. You may only be experiencing a remnant of grief, an unfinished piece.*
14. *Try to put off major decisions.*
15. *Give yourself permission to get professional help.*
16. *Be aware of the pain of your family and friends.*
17. *Be patient with yourself and with others who may not understand.*
18. *Set your own limits and learn to say no.*
19. *Steer clear of people who want to tell you what or how to feel.*
20. *Know that there are support groups which can be helpful, such as The Compassionate Friends or Survivors of Suicide groups. If you can't find a group, ask a professional to help start one.*
21. *Call on your personal faith to help you through.*
22. *It is common to experience physicial reactions to your grief, i.e., headaches, loss of appetite, inability to sleep, etc.*
23. *The willingness to laugh with others and at yourself is healing.*
24. *Wear out your questions, anger, guilt, or other feelings until you can let them go.*
25. *Know that you will never be the same again, but you can survive and go beyond just surviving . . .*

Iris Bolton
TCF, North Atlanta Chapter

CHAPTER VIII

SPECIAL DAYS ARE HARD

I reach for the laughter of Christmas -
Around me are music and light.
The air arches clear into heaven,
A mirror of gold and of white.

I touch it - the laughter of Christmas
The stars are as near as my eyes.
I find in the laughter of Christmas
Your voice, and too many good byes.

Sascha

MOTHER'S DAY

As I write this, I am very much aware that Mother's Day is coming soon. That will be a doubly difficult day in countless homes. For all the thousands of mothers who will be glowing with a radiant kind of pride and happiness on that day, there will also be those of you whose hearts are aching for that phone call that will never come, that special visit, that one Mother's Day card which will not arrive. For us, the reading and rereading of that one last card - "Mom, you are the greatest and I love you" - will have to last a lifetime. How does a mother face a lifetime of silence on "her" day? Ask those of us who have "been there" already, and we will tell you of lonely Mother's Day visits to spring-green cemeteries where the sweet clear notes of a single spring bird perched nearby, float over our heads and seem surely to have been intended as divine comfort for a heart full to breaking. You will hear of yellow roses being sent to a small church - "In memory of..." - and a cherished story of a kind and sensitive friend who sent a single rose that first Mother's Day "in remembrance."

Always we struggle with the eternal question - how does life in fairness exact from us the life of a beloved child in exchange for a clear bird call in a spring-green cemetery, a slender vase of yellow rosebuds or even the kindness and sensitivity of a friend who remembered our loneliness and pain on that day? Where is the fairness and justice of such a barter?

The answer comes back again and again - life does not always bargain fairly. We are surrounded from birth to death by those things which we cannot keep, but which enrich, ennoble and endow our lives with a foretaste of Heaven because we have been privileged to behold, to experience, to wrap our arms around the joyous and the beautiful.

Can we bottle the fragrance of an April morning or the splendor of a winter's sunset and take it home with us to place on our fireplace mantle? Can we grasp and hold the blithesome charm of childhood's laughter? Can we capture within cupped hands the beauty and richness of a rainbow? Can we pluck the glitter of a million stars on a summer night or place in an alabaster box the glow and tenderness of love?

No, we cannot. But to those who have been given the splendor, the blithesome charm, the glory, the glitter, the tenderness and the love of a child who has departed, someday the pain will speak to you of enrichment, of compassion for others, of deeper sensitivity to the world about you, of a deeper joy for having known a deeper pain. Your child will not have left you completely, as you thought. But rather you will find him in that first clear, sweet bird call, in those yellow rosebuds, in giving and in receiving and in the tissue-wrapped memories that you hold forever in your heart.

Mary Wildman
TCF, Moro, IL

OUR DAY . . . A VERY SPECIAL DAY

Our day . . . a very special day. A day that is set aside especially to honor all mothers.

Mother . . . a beautiful word. What other word could you use to best describe giving birth to, nursing, loving and caring for a tiny, helpless human being, a gift of life to treasure? But weren't we taught that once you gave a gift to someone, you should never take it back? What went wrong? Mine was taken away from me. Does that mean that I wasn't worthy to be a mother, that I was failing, that I didn't appreciate the gift? The gift was too precious to be given for keeps. It was only loaned to me for a short while. Even in my sorrow, I feel special, for I know the true meaning of the word ***mother.*** *I have reached the ultimate, from the joy of birth to the sorrow of death. I belong to a special group who truly knows the meaning of the word* ***mother.***

Would I have not accepted the gift if I had known the terrible loss I would feel by having it taken away from me? NO, I would still hold out my hands and accept such a precious gift, for to love and to cherish, even for a short while, is worth every tear.

This year on Mother's Day, I'll shed my tears but let them be as a soft summer's rain - a rain that nourishes the earth, tears that heal and cleanse my heart.

Vera Babb
TCF, St. Louis, MO

PETUNIAS

Petunias in a jelly glass
Held out for me to see
On Mother's Day for 13 years,
My son would give to me.

Petunias bobbing brightly,
They front a graveyard stone
Watered by my salty tears
This Mother's Day alone.

Toni Marx
TCF, Springfield, IL

THE SIGNIFICANCE OF MOTHER'S DAY

I don't think I really appreciated the significance of Mother's Day until I myself became one. My life would never be the same and the death of my only child did not alter the fact that I am still a mother. I still have that intense feeling of love for my child, a love greater than any I had known before. So as Mother's Day approaches, a day on which we recognize the love and pride of motherhood, I, too, want to be remembered as a mother.

Ginny Smith
TCF, Charlottesville, VA

FATHER'S DAY

FATHER'S DAY

Every father believes in his role as protector of his family. He has been assigned the job of fixer and problem solver. He has been told since his youngest days that he must be strong — must not cry.

But each father among us has had to face that point where no amount of fixing, problem solving, and protecting has been able to stop our child's death. And, inside, we must ask ourselves about our failure, and we must face our lack of omnipotence.

Father's Day is often a forgotten holiday, overshadowed by the longer-standing tribute to mothers. But for the bereaved father it is a poignant reminder of bitter sweetness: sweet in the memory of a loved, now lost, child; bitter for the death and pain and recognition of inability to stop what happened.

Fathers do not often have a chance to share their hurts and concerns. Oftentimes they are unable to do so, a remnant of childhood learnings about the strength and stoicism of "big boys." A father may even be uncomfortable opening up to his wife, and the wife who pushes him to talk may be pushing too hard.

Father's Day does not have to be a time when everyone pours out of the woodwork to say, "I'm sorry we haven't talked. Let's do it now." But it can be a time when the family gives Dad a hug, does something special, helps with the chores, and mostly, lets him know how important and needed and loved he is. It is some of these things that he has lost with the death of a child. And, like Mother's Day, the day set aside for fathers does not have to be limited to a Sunday in June. It can be any day and every day.

Fathers often show their hurts differently, often internally. BUT THEY DO HURT.

Gerry Hunt
TCF, White River Junction, VT

MIXED FEELINGS ON FATHER'S DAY

One of the many mixed feelings a father will have on Father's Day will be one of failure - failure as a protector of his child who has died. The roles of protector and father are synonymous. The father's duty is both to love and protect that child from harm. A man may intellectually know he did his best; but the child, his charge, is still painfully absent on this Father's Day.

Dick Moen
TCF, Indianapolis, IN

HURTING ON FATHER'S DAY

As the day approaches
I wonder how I will react -
Am I still a father?
I will sit quietly never
allowing friends and family
to see how I feel.
I miss my son, but I can't
allow myself to "break."
I must remain strong
And always be the "rock."
I wish I could just let
someone know how much I
miss my little angel,
How much I cry and how
much I miss hearing,
"Dad, I love you."
I am a father, but I
wonder will I just pre-
tend, as usual, that
"it doesn't bother me?"
Remember me,
for I hurt, too, on this
special day.

TCF, Tampa. FL

A FATHER'S LOVE MAKES FATHER'S DAY

Father is a solemn person, often deep in thought.
Perhaps its 'cause he seeks for money for the things we've bought.
He may be only dreaming of the things he wished he had
For children that he loves dearly, whether good or bad.

He does desire for Mother that her lot in life improve.
He probably is wishing there were better ways to prove
The love he has for her, "the woman," and for all "the kids."
He may be holding back some tears, just bursting at the lids.

Father does have feelings and is very human too.
There are so many things he wishes he could really do,
For Father loves his family and he wants for them the best,
And yet he cannot let his guard down, act like all the rest.

He must maintain an image and put up a "manly" front.
He must appear to have control and ably bear the brunt
Of problems that the family will so often have to face.
He may apply the discipline when someone's out of place.

Yes, Father is an odd one, yet his heart and hands are kind
And if you search his eyes with care a twinkle you will find
For Father loves the wife and kids more than you'd ever guess.
The family counts the most with Father, he'd have to confess.

So, let's remember Father, though he may be very still,
He cares a a lot for all his folks; concern his heart does fill.
And how he joys as each makes progress, though he may not say!
Still, in his heart he really knows: each day is Father's Day!

Robert F. Gloor
TCF, Tuscaloosa, AL

HALLOWEEN

HALLOWEEN

This month is the time for the little funny-looking creatures appearing at our doors for a trick or treat. Halloween was never my favorite day of the year. I think it was because I could never come up with those cute original costumes for my girls like other mothers managed to do every year. It seemed that after answering the door and seeing two hundred original costumes, I'd always think to myself, "Why didn't I think of that?" I'd tuck a few ideas away in my head for the next year, but when the time came to execute those ideas, I had tucked them so far away I couldn't remember them. Once again we were scrambling around on October 31st trying to come up with ideas that both girls would be happy with. There was six years difference between our two daughters. That wasn't the only difference. Our oldest girl, Kirsten, could have her Halloween candy last until Easter and then we'd throw it out. JoAnn, our youngest, would eat her candy from house to house and would come home with a full stomach and an empty bag.

It was summer when JoAnn had her second open heart surgery. She died on July 2 at age six. When October rolled around that fall, I dreaded that evening of seeing the little children coming to the door and remembering how JoAnn loved the candy and the enthusiasm of the evening. As the evening wore on, I realized that the doorbell wasn't ringing very much. I went to the window and saw that there were plenty of children walking in little groups, but they were walking past our house. I realized then that the neighbors and people who knew us had, no doubt, told the children not to come to our house. My emotions were very mixed up. On one hand, I knew the parents were trying to protect us from this first experience of not having JoAnn. It was very kind of them. On the other hand, it only reminded me of how different our home was now. When nine o'clock came, it was a relief to know the first event was over.

It has been five years now since JoAnn died. Halloween doesn't bother me, but we all know that the next day we turn the calendar and November is here with the holidays around the corner. For us as bereaved parents these are hard times whether you are a newly bereaved parent or have had a number of years since your child died. We need not walk alone; we can reach out to each other. One of the greatest blessings to me now is the gift of memory. I cherish the happy memories of JoAnn in all seasons of the year.

Cindy Holt
TCF, Jamestown, NY

TRICK OR TREAT

The night is dim
And the pumpkins grin
At children on the porch.

The doorbell rings,
"Trick or Treat" they sing.
My heart burns like a torch.

The Dracula's face
And a princess in lace
Are peering in at me.

How I'd love to ask
"May I lift your mask?"
And hiding, there you'd be!

You'd get such a kick
From that silly trick,
But disguised you must stay.

In the wind that blows
My heart still knows
You're playing October charades.

Kathie Slief
TCF, Tulsa, OK

HALLOWEEN MAGIC

Halloween has always been a special holiday time. I regret that our son only had a one-time experience at this magical time of year. I remember - as though it were yesterday - the wonder in his face, how he tried to eat the candy through his mask, how he said thank you without coaxing. Then I think of all the parents whose child never had the opportunity and I am grateful for that one time. It's hard watching all the other children trick-or-treating, and yet there is something special about this season that comforts me. As I watch the trees around me, I am reminded that there is a beauty even in their dying leaves. There's a special aroma, a breathtaking color scheme, and if you listen, a rustling in the air. I believe there is a message in fall. I believe God wants us to know that death is like a change of seasons, that our children now know far more beauty than we can ever imagine. Like the tree that lives on through the barren winter and comes alive again in spring, our children are not gone. They live!

Nancy Cassell
TCF, Monmouth Co., NJ

THANKSGIVING

I remember —
the inability to chew or swallow
that first Thanksgiving after Linda
died;

the choked-back tears, the sick heart,
the hollowness, the painful memories
of Thanksgivings past, and the
blessed relief sleep brought to my
pain.

I remember —
the busyness of working as a volunteer
that second and third Thanksgiving
after Linda died;
and the good feeling it gave me of
"running away" from it all, and the
blessed relief sleep brought to my pain.

I remember —
the inability to prepare any of her
favorite foods that fourth Thanks-
giving after Linda died;
the tears that fell at the smell of
turkey cooking, the parade, football
games, the emptiness, the incomplete
family, and the blessed relief sleep
brought to my pain.

I remember —
awakening with a lightness and joy in
my heart that fifth Thanksgiving
after Linda died;
the thankfulness for having my remaining
family together, the beautiful
memories of past Thanksgivings, the
"wholeness" of me, and the blessed
relief peace brought to my pain.

Priscilla J. Norton
TCF, Pawtucket, RI

SOME SUGGESTIONS FOR THANKSGIVING

Through our lives, expectations of things to come are based upon past experiences. If, in the past, you had set a glorious table and were the perfect host or hostess , it is very possible that friends and family will expect more of the same this year. They may not be aware that you are not looking toward the holidays with a fun and games attitude. They probably do not know that in anticipation of Thanksgiving, Christmas and Channukah, you may feel anxiety and fear. They are probably thinking this year will be different and some sadness will accompany it, but I don't think they are aware of your anguish, especially if it's been "awhile."

I would like to suggest to you that in fairness to yourself you need to be honest about your feelings and, just as important, you need to communicate these feelings to those around you. I really don't think it is necessary for you to believe that because you set a tradition and always made the turkey, fried the latkes, and always had the family over, you need to feel obligated to do it again this year. Perhaps you would like to tell everyone:

- *Someone else will have to make the dinner this year.*
- *You want to make dinner in your home but you need lots of help because you don't have the energy to do it alone.*
- *You want to go to the parties but you are afraid you may break down and cry and you want them to know in advance this is really okay.*
- *You want to tell them it's okay to talk about your child. Not to makes it very uncomfortable*

The list goes on, but the point is that to pretend everything is "just fine" is a lie, and that's not fair to you or to the people who love you.

Diane Zamkoff
TCF, Simi Valley, CA

A TIME OF MEDITATION

Thanksgiving...a time of meditation and thankfulness . . .

Thanksgiving...a time of bitter pain and haunting memories . . . for many a bereaved parent.

"How will we cope with the holiday?" "How will we survive this happy time?" "What is there to be thankful for?"

These questions toss upon our souls, at times, at the very dark times, and taunt us with doubt and fear. Fighting the creeping bitterness, we wait and long for the days of January.

As the years pass, however, the holidays are no longer totally tinged with horror and emptiness. As the acceptance of the death settles in our hearts, the holiday smiles become more genuine. At least some of the warmth returns. But for parents who have only recently (and recently can encompass months and years) suffered the death of a child, the holidays are bleak indeed.

Perhaps the most important thing to remember is that despondency and sorrow at this time of year are normal. What else could be expected of a grieving parent? Joy? Laughter? A sense of overflowing love and outstretched arms? No . . . never.

But as all bereaved parents know, these very emotions, these emotions that are so alien at this time in our lives, are often expected and even demanded. We are not only expected to forget, we are also expected to be filled with joy.

We can refrain from demanding too much of ourselves. We can recognize that at this point we are emotionally exhausted, we are lonely, and we are sad. Maybe we are also angry, guilty and/or bitter. The feelings that arrive with the beginning of a holiday without our beloved sons and daughters are not to be ignored or pushed aside into the corner of our hearts.

By recognizing all of this, we can say "no" to situation or people, even loved friends, who will create more pain. We can cry, silently or loudly, without shame. We can long for the essence of our children and we can remember them with love.

The dreams of lifetimes die when children die. The hurt is often nearly unbearable. But if we allow ourselves the freedom of grief and sorrow, we also open the paths to new happiness and new hopes and new dreams. And the child who was a part of us will live in our memories and our hearts.

I recently read a book about beginnings and endings, depicting how days don't end but night begins, autumn marks the beginning *of winter, and leaves fall from the tree to the ground and feed the earth for new life.*

Death is a final ending to life on earth. For bereaved parents, however, who suffer the pain, the tragedy, the terrible doubts, the ending of a life can be a beginning of new feelings, new understanding and, hopefully, new compassion.

But first we need to follow the instincts of our souls and allow our bodies and hearts to grieve.

TCF, Terre Haute, IN

AT THANKSGIVING

Though you're filled with sorrow and pain over the loss of your child, you can be thankful for —

- *The memories you hold close*
- *The time you shared with your child, no matter how short it was*
- *The things your child taught you*
- *The friends that are there when you need them*

And you can be thankful also for —

- *The strength you have that makes you a survivor*
- *The smiles of other children. They are not our missing children, no, but they still smile.*

TCF, Portland, OR

CHANUKAH

CHANUKAH IS HERE

Chanukah is here.
I see the candles glow,
  red, pink and blue.
But you're not here to
  see their pretty
  shadows.
I shop for gifts.
And this year, again,
  once more,
  I won't be in a quandary
  of what to buy.

I give you my love, my
  precious son,
for that is eternal.

And once again,
it will have to do.

Ginette Kravet
TCF, Central Jersey Chapter

STAR CHILD

Oh Star of David, Star of Light,
shine on all dear children
at Christmas time this night.

I remember the first star you drew,
or think I do.
How you sang the Dreddle Song
"We made it out of clay"
at Hannukkah in Cleveland;
you were seven.

And how your first sentence clearly
said, "Daddy makes the Baby Jesus
house," but the kitten slept in it instead
that first Christmas
in the stonehouse
where we sledded down the snowy
hillside in the moonlight.

We all remember separately,
collectively; around the circle
we hold hands
and breaking, light each candle.

Some say
you watch us from your wall of stars.
Some say you close in close,
complete the ring,
and make the blessing with us,
coming home,
the way we want you to.

Rachell Burrell
TCF, Cincinnati, OH

CHRISTMAS

CHRISTMAS IN BABY HEAVEN

SILENT NIGHT, HOLY NIGHT, ALL IS CALM, ALL IS BRIGHT. Not so, is it? It's the first Christmas since your child's death. It is hell. You find it hard to face the crowded shopping malls; the fa-la-la-la is removed from the decking of the halls; the dancing doll and the ever-so-fast racing sets which glitter of new fallen "create a flake" leave you feeling uneasy; and ole Santa cannot give you what you want most, regardless of how good you are.

Funny, this is the seventh Christmas since your child died and, damn it's not much easier than the first. You still want to rush up and tell the man or the woman with their hands loaded down with Christmas gifts how lucky they are to be buying for their kids. You still want to buy that doll or racing set, but you feel half crazy as you walk into the store. And those Christmas cards are still avoiding the issue, and they hurt, just like they did on the first Christmas.

Perhaps you can and do identify with the paragraphs above. Perhaps your season of glad tidings is a season of hurried tidings. Perhaps the peace on earth hasn't quite found its way into your heart yet. Perhaps your holiday season is filled with avoidance rather than involvement.

In the holidays of joy, why are we so reminded of sadness? Why do we seem to do so well all year long, until Christmas time? Oh, I know you do not need to be reminded that it's particularly a children's holiday and that the windows are so filled with those things that you always wanted to buy for him or her. Maybe it's because it's the season to forget the rational and indulge in our children's fantasy world, only to discover the sea of broken toys on December 26. Maybe it's because it's a season filled with laughter, joy and life. It is a season where the lack of it is disturbingly noticed. It is a season where emptiness becomes emptier and loneliness becomes lonelier. Trapped in this paradox, last Christmas I visited a cemetery off West Florissant Road where children I had known and worked with were buried. The area I visited was particularly significant for it is known as Baby Heaven, that area set aside for the burial of young children.

On that day I almost thought I was at another Compassionate Friends meeting as parents freely mingled and shared among other parents who were visiting their children's gravesites. I sensed an unusual camaraderie in that other parents had a real sense of what the others were going through. It was as though each was telling the other that "you are not alone."

After a while many couples (and a large number of children of all ages) departed, and I took the liberty of visiting the graves. The ensuing twenty minutes I will never forget. There lay the spirit of Christmas, as if the area was under a huge Christmas tree. There was the big red drum with the words, "We miss you, Robbie" on the top. And Amanda has "Tiny Tearful," the crying doll, next to her tombstone. A teddy bear, a tin soldier, and manger scenes helped to fill the cemetery toyland. Another child's family had Christmas cards, complete with personal messages in each, paper-clipped into the ground. And, of course, there were numerous decorated Christmas trees with ornaments made by the surviving siblings - sad, yet beautiful.

I walked away and tried to gather my emotions. My psychological side began yelling out various and unimportant theories, conclusions, and abstracts; my personal side found peace. What I indeed saw was beauty in the midst of tragedy. I saw families remembering their children in special, real ways. They had not put their deceased child into a special role, but allowed the child's role to remain special. The grave decorations did not make the deceased children untouchable saints, but allowed them to be the memory of what they really were - good but not perfect children.

What I saw that day will stay with me forever for I saw expressions of giving, expressions of Christmas. I saw the hope in parents' eyes, the same hope found in a child's eyes as they awake Christmas morning to discover that Santa has arrived. And perhaps that is what God had in mind when he sent His son to us on a Christmas morning two thousand years ago - hope, understanding, and the feeling that He is with us always.

And so, this Christmas I encourage you to visit your child's gravesite. Allow Christmas to happen there as it happens in your home. Allow the givingness inside of you to give once more. God bless you. Have a hope-filled Christmas.

SILENT NIGHT, HOLY NIGHT, ALL IS SOMEWHAT CALM, ALL IS SOMEWHAT BRIGHT.

Larry Siedle
(Pastoral counselor at Cardinal
Glennon Hospital for children)
TCF, St. Louis, MO Newsletter

AS WE NEAR THE SPECIAL SEASON

As we near the special season that stirs up feelings of heritage, patriotism, thanksgiving, and our relationship with God, we are instantly reminded that it doesn't seem to fit together for us; our personal sense of well-being is suffering. Our hearts and spirits are undergoing the trauma of painfully fresh wounds in some cases, while others are coping with the scar tissue of older grief that refuses to heal or restore comfort to their lives. This season reminds me we are living with extra stress that must be resolved. I offer a few thoughts to each of you, along with my love, in hope that feelings of peace and purpose will return to bring you comfort.

First, be careful in agreeing to take on the traditional extra work that goes with holidays. You are coping with grief that will take much of your usable energy.

Second, be especially kind and patient with yourself. The need for physiological rest is vital at this time; regular sleep and rest hours will help.

Third, be aware that holidays and alcohol have become traditional companions; extra caution may be necessary to prevent the depressant effects of alcohol from further aggravating your grief anxiety

Fourth, it's okay to change past practices that are especially painful reminders of what can be no more; do something different if you have to.

Finally, allow yourself private time as you need to, but also remember it's important to allow others to try to bring you comfort and give you extra help during the holidays. Loved ones need feedback that says: "I'm trying to recover, and I appreciate your help." Peace be with you.

Ann Frost
TCF, Middle Georgia Chapter

PROGRESS HANDLING CHRISTMAS

It was the third holiday season after my son died, and I was not yet sure what kind of Christmas it was going to be for me. As I stood in a department store line waiting to pick up a package, behind me in line, two women, strangers to each other, struck up a conversation having to do with the usual complaints that surface around the holiday season.

Each laden with packages, the two women began complaining (but not really) about how much too long their children's lists were, as usual. They compared how hard it had been to find "it" - whatever the in-thing was for boys and girls that year, about how tired they were, and about how different it was going to be next year. Their complaints were superficial, and you knew next year would be no different as they went about trying to fulfill as many dreams as was possible.

Had this been the year before, or the one before that, these mothers would have probably regretted being in line behind me, for I would have had a need to punish them for their innocence and good luck, to remind them, unnecessarily I'm sure, how fortunate they were to have their children alive to buy for. I would have made them feel guilty for having done some good-natured complaining. Instead, this year I realized as I listened quietly that though I envied them their innocence and complacency, I had no need to punish them for my misfortune. Can you see how far I had come in a year? Some of my anger and frustration had subsided, and I didn't need to punish.

As I left, I wished them both a Merry Christmas and silently thanked them for helping me discover what kind of Christmas it was going to be for me. I had made progress, but it had taken a year and this particular scenario for me to be able to judge it. I still missed my boy, but I was getting better.

If you don't have progress to recognize this year, maybe next year? I hope so.

Mary Cleckley
TCF, Atlanta, GA

CHRISTMAS - A DIFFICULT TIME

The holiday period is an especially difficult time for bereaved parents and particularly for the newly bereaved. The holidays, which have been our happiest times with our children, are a time when the changes that tragedy has made in our lives are most evident. As we gather our emotional forces to make a happy day for surviving children, grandparents, and other family members, it can be a very difficult time.

It helps to know that you will find the holidays less difficult than your fear of them and you will find some of your happy memories, too. Our children live on in our memories and in the many happy holiday times now past.

We hope that during this period you can find some happy times to remember and to cherish. We were fortunate to have had these wonderful children as long as we did, and we will have our memories of the good times they enjoyed.

The pain of loss will always be there. We share that, and we have a special concern for those who are having their first holidays without their children. There will be hard times and sad days. Without grief, there would be nothing. In that grief there are some wonderful memories to cherish. We will be with you in spirit. You are not alone.

Dayton Robinson
TCF, Tuscaloosa, AL

A LETTER TO MY FAMILY AND FRIENDS

Thank you for not expecting too much from me this holiday season.

It will be our first Christmas without our child and I have all I can do coping with the "spirit" of the holiday on the radio, tv, in the newspapers and stores. We do not feel joyous, and trying to pretend this Christmas is going to be like the last one will be impossible because we are missing one.

Please allow me to talk about my child if I feel a need. Don't be uncomfortable with my tears. My heart is breaking and the tears are a way of letting out my sadness.

I plan to do something special in memory of my child. Please recognize my need to do this in order to keep our memories alive. My fear is not that I'll forget, but that you will.

Please don't criticize me if I do something that you don't think is normal. I'm a different person now and it may take a long time before this different person reaches an acceptance of my child's death.

As I survive the stages of grief, I will need your patience and support, especially during these holiday times and the "special" days throughout the year.

Thank you for not expecting too much from me this holiday season.

Love,
A bereaved parent
TCF, Madison, WI

THE NEW YEAR

FOR THE NEW YEAR

Instead of the old kind of New Year's resolutions we used to make and break, let's make some this year and really try to keep them.

1. *Let's not try to imagine the future - take one day at a time.*
2. *Allow yourself time to cry, both alone, and with your loved ones.*
3. *Don't shut out other family members from your thoughts and feelings. Share these difficult times. You may all become closer for it.*
4. *Try to be realistic about your expectations - of yourself, your spouse, other family members and friends. Each of us is an entity, therefore different. So how can there be perfect understanding?*
5. *When a good day comes, relish it; don't feel guilty and don't be discouraged because it doesn't last. It WILL come again and multiply.*
6. *Take care of your health. Even though the mind might not care, a sick body will only compound your troubles. Drink lots of water and take stress-type multivitamins, rest (even if you don't sleep), and get moderate exercise. Help your body heal, as well as your mind.*
7. *Share your feelings with other Compassionate Friends and let them share with you. As you find you are caring about the pain of others, you are starting to come out of your shell - a very healthy sign.*

I know following these won't be easy but what has been? It's worth a try, don't you think? Nothing to lose and perhaps much to gain.

Mary Ehmann
TCF, Valley Forge,PA

THIS CAN BE A CONSTRUCTIVE, IF NOT A HAPPY YEAR

HAPPY NEW YEAR??? "How can it ever be again?" "How will I ever make it through another year of this torment?"

When we are hurting and so terribly depressed, it is hard to see any good in our new year, but we must try. First, we must hold on tightly to the idea that we will not always be this miserable, that we will some day feel good again. This is almost impossible to believe, but even if we don't believe it, we must tell ourselves over and over again that IT IS TRUE - BECAUSE IT IS! Many parents whose children have died in the past will attest to this. Remember also, no one can suffer indefinitely as you are suffering now.

Second, we must face the new year with the knowledge that this year offers us a CHOICE - whether we will be on our way to healing this time next year or still be in the pit of intense grief. We must remind ourselves that if we choose to be on our way to healing by the following year, we must work to get there and that work entails allowing ourselves to go through our grief, to cry, to be angry, to talk about our guilts, to do whatever is necessary to move towards healing.

Third, we must look for good in our lives and find reasons to go on and accept the fact that our continued suffering will not bring our child back. Many of us have other children and a spouse for whom we must go on. More important, we have our own lives that must be lived. Most of us know that our dead children would want us to go on!

No, this coming year may not be a happy one, but it can be a constructive one. Through our grief we can grow and become more understanding, loving, compassionate, and aware of the real values in life. LET US NOT WASTE THIS NEW YEAR.

Margaret H. Gerner
TCF, St. Louis, MO

FOR THE NEW YEAR

Where there is pain,
let there be softening
Where there is bitterness,
let there be acceptance
Where there is silence,
let there be communication
Where there is loneliness,
let there be friendships
Where there is despair,
let there be hope.

Ruth Eiseman
TCF, Louisville, KY

THAT FIRST NEW YEAR

Over and over again I have looked at this picture of bells ringing in the Happy New Year.

The first New Year after Tom died I remember wondering if we could survive this tragedy in our lives and ever be a normal family again. We had just muddled through Christmas - and made it - and now we were starting a new year. We were still picking up the pieces in our lives. Other people who had experienced the death of a child told us "it would get better," "time helps heal the sorrow." At the time, I didn't see how it could. I thought, "It's okay for them to talk, to tell us these things, but we're never going to really get our heads on straight again!"

After that first year things DID get better. What they said really did happen - time does help the healing process. Of course, the memories will always be part of our lives because we never want to forget him.

Lorraine Bauman
TCF, Fairmont, MN

TO START A NEW YEAR

If I can concentrate
on the moral and spiritual
side of the holidays
I can make it through.

If I can absorb
the love and warmth
that was the beginning
I can give love back.

If I can share
the grief and the love
that is in me
through these holidays
I can start a new year.

Tom Spray
TCF, Ventura County, CA

CHAPTER IX

SEASONS CHANGE AND SO DO WE

Look to the season of your memories —
it fills the weather of your life
with mildness.
It turns to laughter what your
mind remembers:
the sound of words invented new,
for singing,
discovery of all-important secrets.

Look to the season of your memories —
it sets an ordinary past to music.
It changes ordinary tears to treasure.
It gives your faded pictures
shape and color:
the touch of eyes, a walk
in foggy twilight.

Look to the seasons of your memories —
how rich you were, and be how rich again.
Look to the season of your memories:
mourn and enjoy the child you love,
you love —
and you will loose yourself
to find yourself.

Sascha

WINTER

A WORD ABOUT WINTER

Winter will shortly be upon us, bringing with it many fluctuating emotions. Winter is a time of bareness and coldness which often leaves us feeling the same way. It seems as if the joy and warmth of spring and summer are fading away and the dreariness of winter is strong upon us. But winter doesn't have to be cold and barren if we don't want it to. We can overcome the dread of winter in many ways. We can still have the joy and warmth of spring and summer though the world around us is bare and cold

We can warm our hearts and have the joy we deserve by reflecting on the precious and loving moments with our children. Though we may feel sadness, those memories can fill us with an unending flood of warmth and love. They can warm us and bring us joy even on the bitterest cold days and nights.

Talking and reaching out to other bereaved parents can also bring us relief and joy. We can share memories of our children, our feelings, and find release from our dreary moments. We don't have to be cold and barren if we don't want to—the choice is ours.

Just as winter fades away and God once again whispers the promise of a rose, so will our pain and despair lessen and pass, and we will once again have contentment, peace and joy in our lives. Sadness may drift in once in awhile, but we can overcome it and let the sunshine of our being and joy come bounding through. So during this winter, let us hold onto the promise of that rose and along with it, a lessening sense of pain and sorrow. God be with you and comfort you during this winter.

Deborah Wells,
TCF, Baltimore, MD

LIKE A TREE IN WINTER

Like a tree in winter
which has lost its leaves,
we look ahead to spring
for new growth and the warmth
of the sun to heal the pain in our hearts.

Let us make January a time
to reach out to each other
and give that warmth from our hearts,
and in return,

We will all show new growth.

Pat Dodge
TCF, Sacramento Valley, CA

CAN SPRING BE FAR BEHIND?

On Groundhog Day we watch to see if that creature will see its shadow, an omen of six more weeks of winter. At that point I think many of us are weary of the cold weather and are looking forward to spring. Spring is a renewal and revitalization of nature after a cold, hard winter. We delight in seeing the first crocus, the first robin. With the arrival of spring in March, even though we may still have blustery winds, there is the promise of something new in the air. We look forward to the wearing of the green on St. Patrick's Day, the egg hunts for the children and the Easter parade.

But wait, is all this true for all of us, especially for the newly bereaved parent? When a child dies, no matter what season it may be at that time, for the parents it may be a cruel and harsh winter. The day may be radiant, the sky blue, the weather balmy, but for these parents the "winter of our discontent" may be long, difficult and protracted. We are so shattered in our grief that even changing seasons may seem to us as one. But by the law of nature, even the most brutal winter must pass and a more gentle and compassionate climate take its place. Wasn't it Shelley who wrote, "If winter comes, can spring be far behind?"

Dave Ziv
TCF, Bucks Mont Chapter, PA

SPRING

SEASONS CHANGE AND SO DO WE

These warm days remind us spring is here and summer is coming. Some of us, as bereaved parents, stare at the yard and think: "Where will the energy come from to prune and plant one more time now that our child is dead?"

Spring is a time of renewal, nature's loving promise of eternal life. So many things about our child will never die - the light in young eyes that came with a smile, the warmth of a hug, the joy we experienced as we watched the child discover and grow. These things came from love - our love and our child's love. Is there a way to take back love or the memories of it? Once experienced, love is eternal, just as the awakening of each season occurs over and over and will always do so.

We can do some things even in our state of depleted energy. Touching growing things can rejuvenate a battered heart. Try planting a small flower bed or a pot of special flowers in memory of your child. Tend it with love and watch it respond. It will give you pleasure and a closeness with your child you can experience in no other way. The strength to face your bereavement will grow with the plants.

One of our members planted a rose garden in memory of her son. She speaks of how much she enjoys looking at the roses outside and bringing them in. Tending the rose garden is a special act of love, an act of cherishing.

Planting, tending, and enjoying is a salute to our child and to the way the world is planned for eternal renewal and change. Perhaps it says we don't have the energy to recover all at once, so we will care for these tender plants as we heal. Healing is not instantaneous, even for a limb pruned by the clippers. When grass is moved down, it's not back to its original height in the morning. If nature heals slowly, maybe this is the way set up for us, too.

Each season invites us to experience its cycle, its pattern which, while it involves change and, yes, even death, is a promise that as one stage of our lives turns into another, there can be beauty and joy mixed in with pain and loss. We do not believe when the trees bare themselves in the fall, there will never be green leaves again. So with the arrival of yet another cycle, touch, see, smell, taste, and perhaps enjoy nature's renewal. The eternal cycles are a promise that nothing ever goes away permanently. They speak to us of strength for change and immortality - our own and our child's.

Elizabeth B. Estes
TCF, Augusta, GA

SPRINGTIME'S BURDEN BECOMING PROMISE

Seasonal changes are difficult for many bereaved parents. This is often most true as winter yields to spring.

The land seems to throb with life once more as young buds emerge and robins return from their sojourn in the south. Lilacs bloom and the breeze carries their fragrance. Woodland animals begin to lose the leanness of winter hunting or quiet hibernation.

The day is longer and filled with renewed vitality to match its length. It is as if a cold hand had loosed its bitter grip and the earth is reborn.

It is this quality of resurrection that seems so bitter. For as we struggle in the darkness of loss, all around us is the vigorous rush of life breaking forth in colors and song. But our children do not come forth. They dwell in the land of death and the netherworld nightmares of our anguish.

But I believe we can see as well the promise inherent in spring's unfolding glory and grasp the continuity its return affirms. Last fall we saw an acorn, but this year we see the tender shoot of an infant tree. From gnarled, dead-looking stumps, the cut-back rose sends tendrils of green to drink the sun.

In each full cycle of our planet around its sun, we encounter irrefutable testament to renewal. In this we sense the defeat of death. This is the time of year, when twilight surrenders to darkness, to stand outside and feel the rays of countless stars, smell the scents granted by the new earth, hear the chorus of night creatures and sense the rebirth that has no end.

Stand silently then, beneath the constancy of the night sky and upon the rejuvenating earth, and sense our children, constant and growing too, yet beyond our sight. Life continues. There are no endings. There are only beginnings. That is the promise of spring.

Don Hackett
TCF, South Shore, MA

THRESHOLD

Every year I am shocked by spring.
Here it comes suddenly, like a curtain
made of colorful print material, dropping,
transforming the land.

Each year
I feel like I haven't been paying attention.
One morning I wake and my world is gaudy with color,
giddy - like someone shook the champagne
and it spilled, its effervescence
waking the flowers early, drunk and in love.

There is no memory of the neon leaves of fall.
Winter's wind has pushed on.
I'm glad it's gone.
It had become a guest who stayed too long,
a bore that drove me to my room.

Each year when the azaleas bloom,
I remember another spring.
That one wore a pall.
The rain would not stop. It poured
into the open grave of my son.
It poured deep into my heart.
I was sure it would never,
ever,
stop.

It did,
though I sometimes wished it hadn't.
I was stuck between forgetting
and remembering.
Remembering won.
Now I see his face in the azaleas.
They bloomed that spring
while he died.

I no longer hold it against them.

Fay Harden
TCF, St. Louis Newsletter

SPRING

I'm afraid of the spring.
I'm afraid, you might say,
Of other children's voices
As they come out to play.

I'm afraid of the feelings
Deep down in my heart;
With all the pain and the hurt
I may fall apart.

Shall I shut all the windows
So I don't hear a thing?
Shall I shut my eyes
So I can't see spring?

Shall I let winter live
The whole year through?
And feel safer inside
And a lot colder too?

Penny Lenehan
TCF, Brookside, NJ

SUMMER

SUMMER THOUGHTS

Summer is a time when things naturally slow down, a time when many are waiting for the orderly routine of their lives to begin again. For those of us in grief whose lives are already in limbo, it can seem endless if we let it. Seeing children, babies, and teenagers is not easy for us, and in summer we see them everywhere from shopping centers to beaches. Everyone is out living, loving, enjoying carefree activities with their children, and we want to scream, "It's not fair!"

I was sitting on my patio one evening at dusk recently listening to the shouts of children outside playing, and I was crying as I remembered the sounds that my child used to make. I became very depressed as I thought what a long summer this was going to be.

In my reverie I was reminded of a recent comment I had heard at a TCF meeting: "My child was such a loving, giving person. He would not want me to waste my life being bitter." I also remembered a good friend telling me to "count my blessings" and naming over all the things I had to be grateful for. I was furious at the time. Nothing that I had to be grateful for could compensate for the fact that my child was dead.

Now, sitting in the twilight of this early summer evening, I began to see things differently. I determined that this summer would not be an eternity, that I would not let it be. I decided first of all to stay busy. I know I can find plenty to do if I only take the time to look. I am also going to try to enjoy the simple things that used to give me so much pleasure, like working in my garden and flowers. I then decided to try to be truly grateful for the blessings that I have, like my husband, my surviving children, my job, friends, etc.

It has been almost five years for me, and I know that last year this would not have worked. Of course, I still have times of sadness. I know I always will, but I have decided that in the process of grieving, we close so many doors that the only way to recovery is to reopen them gradually at our own pace.

I know I will never be the same person I was before the death of my child, but I hope eventually in some ways I will be a better person because suffering can be beneficial if we learn and grow through it. A year ago I didn't feel this way, and I know I still have a long way to go, but in the meantime I know the greatest tribute to my child will be to enjoy this summer as he would have done.

Libby Gonzalez
TCF, Huntsville, AL

GRIEF AND VACATION TIME

Vacation time, like holidays, can be especially painful for bereaved parents. Caught up with normal demands of making a living or keeping a household going, we have less time to think than we do on vacations, especially the "take it easy" kind at a hideaway tucked away somewhere.

In the summers following Tricia's death, I found vacations could bring a special kind of pain. We avoided going to locales where we had vacationed with her. At one time, I thought Williamsburg might be off my list forever since we had an especially happy holiday there with her and her younger sister. I tried it one summer three years later and found that she walked the cobbled streets with me. Now that nine years have elapsed and the searing pain has eased, maybe I can let the happy memories we shared in Williamsburg heighten the pleasure of another visit there.

For the first few years after Tricia's death, we found fast-paced vacations to be best at places we had never been before. The sheer stimulation of new experiences in new places with new people refreshed us and sent us home more ready to pick up our grief work. That is not to say when we did something or saw something that Tricia would have particuarly enjoyed, we didn't mention her. We did, but it seemed less painful than at home. One caution: do allow enough time for sleep. Otherwise, an exhausted body will depress you.

Charles and I have found that an occasional separate vacation (or weekend) is helpful. This, too, is an opportunity to change our stride, to experience the world a little differently. One experimentation with this may have stemmed from a reevaluation of priorities. Life is too short to miss a trip associated with a special interest. A writer's workshop that might bore Charles is no longer off limits to me, any more than his going alone to a postal convention. Allow yourself space since you are not grieving at the same rate. When I go by myself, I take only my memories, not his and mine, and my response to them is different. I have often found this helps straighten out my thinking.

We've said it a hundred times: you have to find your own way, your own peace. Let vacation time be another try at that, but do give yourself a break in choosing the time and locale where that can be accomplished. Don't be afraid of change; it helps with your reevaluation of life.

Elizabeth B. Estes
TCF, Augusta, GA

WHERE DID THE SUMMER GO?

The days are now long and hot! Summer is already half gone and at times I wonder where the time has gone! There was a time three years ago when I thought the days would never pass, that the warm days were mocking me in my grief. It was very hard to get out of bed in the morning, only to face the long day ahead till night when sleep could ease my hurt for a short while. Our son loved the outdoors and summer and would rather be outside than eat. It was hard to get him in at night. In fact, we would, and still do, refer to a really bright, summer day as a "Chrissy Day." But this made it very hard to enjoy the nice weather with all the children outside laughing and playing.

I stayed inside most of those first two summers, not being able to enjoy the days. It was easier, it seemed to me, than to face it all. But as time went by I found I was really missing the warmth of the sun on my face and the summertime laughter of children. Not that I missed Chris less, just that I was able to remember the fun things without hours of crying and pain.

Three years ago I would not have believed this possible, but I have "survived" and can now see other blond, blue-eyed, brown-bodied little boys riding their big wheels and not fall apart. I'm not saying it doesn't hurt, but the sharp stabs come and go very quickly now and I can remember Chris for a moment and then go on to enjoy the summer with my family and friends. Believe me, I've been there. It does get better with time. You don't ever forget, but you find out that, indeed, life does go on if you want it to.

Please try to enjoy the summer as best you can. Take each day as it comes and live through that one. I know it will be very hard for you newly bereaved parents, but take it from someone who has had three summers, it will get easier and someday you will say, "Where did the summer go?"

Darlene Virtue
TCF, Memphis, TN

END OF SUMMER

Remembrance of a little boy at the ocean
—by his mother

On the beach, cool breezes blow across the water, but the sun's rays feel warm upon my face. The ocean laps gently at the shore. One golden haired lad I spy with shovel and pail filling the moat around his lovingly constructed sand castle.

I remember another golden haired boy of years long past, in his bright red swim suit, busy at his task and oblivious to all around him. Carefully, patiently, he fills and empties his pail again and again - molding and shaping the sand until he has it just right, until his perfect castle is completed. He runs to me, eyes aglow with pride, his dimpled smile stretched from ear to ear. He dances around me. "Mommy, come see - it's finished - it's perfect." We stand and admire it together - one bucket of sand turned down, a tiny trench encircling it. To us it is a perfect castle.

But then it happens. A wave, much bigger than the rest, washes away his labor of love. His green eyes fill, his lip quivers momentarily and then he squares his shoulders and announces, "Oh well, I'll begin again tomorrow."

And now, recalling that other sunny summer day, my own eyes brimming with tears, my own lip quivers until I remember that I, too, can square my shoulders and begin again tomorrow.

Betty Stevens
TCF, Baltimore, MD

AUTUMN

SEPTEMBER

September brings such joy and such sorrow. I enjoy shopping with Travis for school clothes - even though each year it means all new jeans, shirts and shoes. What a joy! He has grown taller and it's a pleasure to watch him change from his first kindergarten days to this year's maturing fourth grader. And always, each year, I wonder about Jesse. When we're out shopping and I see that certain shade of green, my heart skips a beat or two - how he would have liked that shirt! And I think of what a pleasure it would be to watch him change, too, from year to year.

And I wonder would he think he was too old (II years) for a lunch pail this year? Would he want to buy his lunch? He never liked to buy it; he always wanted to take his own lunch pail, but after all he was just six.

September...full of joys and sorrows...full of memories. Now they must last a lifetime. Always in my heart and mind, now and forever, even though Jess isn't with us, he's still our son, our child, a wonderful, precious joy, a gift from God, too soon gone home!!

Kathy Barker
TCF, Sacramento, CA

AUTUMN

In the fall
When amber leaves are shed,
Softly—silently
Like tears that wait to flow,
I watch and grieve.

My heart beats sadly
In the fall;
'Tis then I miss you
Most of all.

Lily de Lauder
TCF, Van Nuys, CA

SEPTEMBER SONG

I wonder how many people think about what it's like for a parent not to have to pack a Snoopy lunch pail for their child ever again.

September marks the reentry of kids into the world of academia, but for some parents it's the reminder that the excitement of the children that electrifies the air won't be the same in their home this year. So many hopes and dreams and memories are wrapped up in what occupies a major part of a child's life - school time. Summer cushions us from having to be painfully aware that our child won't be walking to school with the other kids or won't be trying out for the lead part in the school play or won't need new school clothes or won't fall in love with the girl he sits behind in math class.

Parents who never had the pleasure of "letting them go" to school for the first time know what they missed. They remember their own "first time" and would have liked to have relived it with their child. They would have liked to have made it really special and to have asked all the questions their own parents asked them when they arrived home from school. Hopes and dreams for this child's future will never be realized. I wonder if my neighbor remembers that if my baby had lived, this is the year he would have started kindergarten. I wanted him to have a Snoopy lunch box just like the other kids.

TCF, Portland, OR

AUTUMN FEELINGS

During the next couple of months we will see many changes taking place in the world around us. The amount of daylight is decreasing; nights are becoming chilly; we'll often need sweaters or jackets as we venture forth each day. However, the most dramatic change that we notice here in New England during September and October is that of the trees trading their green summer outfits for the brilliant red, oranges and golds of autumn.

Many of us who are bereaved parents find ourselves feeling tense and depressed when the earth awakens in the spring; we may also experience these feelings when the dramatic changes of autumn occur.

A wise lady once said to me, "Our bodies respond to the changing seasons." She was right. They do! And they respond by FEELING. It seems to me that all of the grief feelings that I have - emptiness, sadness, anger, loneliness, guilt, depression - are intensified as the world of nature around me changes.

Sometimes, however, we can draw strength from situations that seem on the surface to be negative. A few weeks after Linda's death I heard from two friends within a few days of each other. One said, "You know, when I'm troubled, I get out and walk until I find something in nature that I've never seen before. I look at it and think about it, and I am renewed."

The other friend, who has some physical disabilities, wrote me a note in which she said, "Whenever I feel discouraged, I find something in nature to study, and I am renewed."

I think that hearing from these two friends within just a few days of each other had to be more than a coincidence. I feel that there was an important message there for me, and I've tried to act on it.

I can draw strength from an early morning walk, from frost patterns on our windows, from a raging blizzard, from birds at our feeder, from a rainbow, a ladybug or a whale - if I slow down, think about those things, observe their intricacy and beauty, and attempt to let some of their energy into myself.

We have to slow down, try to realize what is happening to us and be receptive to the energy that is in the natural world for us. When I'm down because it's a sparkling clear, colorful autumn day and Linda isn't here to experience it with me, I have to feel that pain, then let it go so that the natural beauty and energy around me can strengthen and renew me.

Let yourself experience autumn - the emptiness and aching that you feel. Then try to let go of those feelings just enough to let the wonder and beauty of the season into yourself - one day at a time.

Evelyn Billings
TCF, Springfield, MA

CHAPTER X

DREAMS AND UNUSUAL HAPPENINGS ARE A PART OF HEALING, TOO

At a Concert (with Eve?)

Just by chance
the seat beside me
is an empty seat.
And my mind starts dreaming . . .

You are next to me,
and at the andante
you nudge me gently:
you look at me
with half a smile,
then you close your eyes
and pantomime a sigh —
we understand each other . . .

But the seat beside me
is an empty seat.

Sascha

DREAMS - SUBCONSCIOUS AIDS TO GRIEF RESOLUTION

Dreams and unusual happenings are a natural part of our human experience. They are important in bringing us messages about ourselves; it is important to give them our full attention when we need and want to learn from them.

Each of us is irreversibly linked to every other human being who has preceded us in history. What our ancestors felt, thought, and believed in is an indelible part of our present psychic experience. Our ancestral history is part of the collective history of mankind. This collective history creates a symbolic repository from which we draw on a nightly basis as we create our dreams. Consequently, each dream presents us with images which are both personally unique and universally human.

The word ***psyche****, which is Greek in origin, is the expression we use for all the thought processes and symbolic experiences we have that are part of our conscious thoughts, our unconscious processes, and that area in-between that is accessible to us at some times, but not always. The conscious part of the psyche is ego or "I-ness." Our ego works diligently in its attempts to maintain a non-threatening psychological and spiritual state. The unconscious is fluid and unwilling to yield to the rigidity of the ego. The unconscious brings us memories, feelings, images, dreams, etc. to assist us with our psychological and our spiritual growth. Dreams are one way the psyche attempts to provide the ego with balance for its rigidity.*

Why do we have recurring dreams? They are natural and normal experiences and are almost always telling us one of two things. First, that we have an unfinished piece of inner work: something keeps bubbling up and reminding us of the inner work to do done. Second, it may be that we've had an experience so healing that we keep repeating it through our dreams in order to continue the process.

What about nightmares? Although nightmares may frighten us, they are 90% pure gold. Because of their vividness, we don't forget the story. They are an attempt of the unconscious to paint a picture of something that the unconscious insists that the ego allow into consciousness. They do not require, need, or benefit from a literal interpretation. In dealing with a nightmare, it is helpful to share it with someone as soon as possible. If possible, write it down; let the unconscious know that you take the message seriously. Often this alone will reduce the need to keep getting attention from the ego in this way. After a nightmare, perform some small ritual such as turning on the light, getting up and moving about in order to enable you to think about your dream in a normal everyday, nonthreatening setting. This allows you to move the experience from a fearful experience that you don't care to look at, to a natural experience that is part of your inner work. After a nightmare, a glass of milk can serve as a natural tranquilizer to help you calm down.

Why can't you dream about your child? You do. It is wonderful when we dream and see our child's face, but we dream about our child in other ways as well. Dreams are pictures; they are spiritual poetry. Symbolically, through our dreams we paint pictures and write poetry that must be understood and absorbed in a different way. When you dream, write it down; it can also be helpful to draw the images and make note of colors. Then begin to look at what the dream describes for you. For example, you may have a dream about the color pink; then you recall the pink draperies in your daughter's room, the pink on her birthday cake, the pink barrettes she asked you to buy. You are dreaming of your child.

When you dream, your child may not be directly in the dream, but somewhere on the periphery. When it feels right to you, go back to your dream in the daytime, in a quiet place where you can relax. Go back to your dream and invite your child to come forward. Talk to him/her in a normal, natural way. Trust your inner work to continue when you are in a relaxed atmosphere. Trust the gift you are giving yourself. Be open to the experience as you remember, grieve and release some of your grief. If possible, find someone who can work with you during this time.

Can we influence what we dream about? Some have found that when, just before going to sleep, they review mentally the things they would like to dream about, they then experience in their dreams things related to the subjects they yearn to dream about. For others this does not work. We don't know why there are differences of experience.

Through dreams, many people find that they can write things (poetry, for example), say things, experience things that they have not been able to before. Our human capacity is much greater than we suspect, not through our conscious ego, but through our unconscious spirit.

Excerpts from a taped presentation
by Paula Reeves, PhD, Atlanta, Ga.
given at our National Conference.

THE SINGLE MOST MEMORABLE HOLIDAY I'VE EVER HAD

I am not writing here to sadden anyone, but as a tribute to LOVE, FAMILY, and FAITH. On 6 December 1985 my daughter, Michelle, was murdered. While gathering her things to bring home, we found Michelle had lovingly made Christmas gifts for everyone in the family. Family came from Florida, Canada, Arizona and here in Georgia and remained through the holidays.

Sometime before the incident, my daughter told me that she had a dream that the whole family was together at Christmas time and she was outside the window looking in. She said that in her dream she felt such a feeling of contentment at seeing us all together. It had been years since all of the family had been together.

We decided to have Christmas as Michelle would have wanted it. My husband and I wrapped the gifts Michelle had so lovingly made for those she loved. On Christmas morning, while we were opening the gifts, my husband told me to look out the window. There are two rocking chairs on the porch and one was rocking back and forth. My husband reached over and held my hand, and it was at that moment I remembered what Michelle had told us about her dream, and I realized then that her dream had become a reality. Michelle was still with all of us and was indeed content at watching the family she loved so much sharing the joy of Christmas together.

I also realized Michelle would always be watching me and that, though in one sense she had been taken from us, she would always be a part of all of us. The little gifts she made for everyone that Christmas would be treasured for many Christmases to come, but what would be treasured most was her LOVE OF FAMILY and the FAITH of knowing that one day we will be together again.

Ann Marie Parman
TCF, Augusta, GA

THE TURNING POINT

Some months after my son died I found myself wondering if I could ever find purpose and meaning in my loss. Would my turning point ever come? Oh! how I missed him. Then it came. I believe there is a turning point for every bereaved parent if you desire for there to be one. It comes in different ways for each of us if we are to be "survivors" in the fullest sense of the word. It may come in a sunrise; it may come through another child who needs you; it may come at an altar in prayer. There are thousands of ways it may come - BUT IT MUST COME. Mine came in a dream.

There he was! Walking toward me as if coming out a mist. There he was - that lanky 17-year-old whose life I loved better than my own. He looked deeply into my eyes with a grin on his face, the way he used to do when he was "buttering me up." Not a word was spoken, but everything was said that needed to be said for my turning point to come.

It was time to resume life. I would not be bitter, but in loving memory I would be better. I would live again because I knew that my boy lived again. My own Christian faith was to be retrofitted. It offered meaning and purpose within the shadow of my loss. It asserted that though God does not intend my sufferings, He involves Himself in them. My pain and loss were not to be the end of life. Rather, it was to be a beginning - a beginning to a more compassionate life of quality and caring.

His bear hug told me, "It's okay. Go ahead and live life in its fullness as a tribute to me." Thank you, David; that's the greatest gift a son could ever give to his dad.

Rev. Ken Kulp
TCF, Atlanta, GA

BUTTERFLIES AND VISIONS

The daughter of a friend of mine was killed in an auto crash a short time ago. In one of our telephone conversations she hesitantly told me that her surviving son had "a vision" of his sister. I could tell the way she was telling the story that she wasn't sure just how I would react. She told me her son is an intelligent and stable person and wouldn't make up something like this. I could almost hear the relief in her voice when I told her that his experience is not an unusual one; a large number of grieving people report similar experiences.

Actually, nearly half of the grieving population have a sensory experience that involves their deceased loved one. Grievers report seeing, hearing or strongly feeling their loved one's presence. Others report an event or occurrence that assures them that their loved one is safe and happy.

Various theories attempt to explain this phenomenon, but none are conclusive. For those of us who have had these experiences, the only important conclusion we need is that the experience was very real and very meaningful to us. You may be able to explain the presence of a purple butterfly over the grave of my three-year-old granddaughter one sunny afternoon, but for me it was a message from Emily saying: "Grandma, I'm okay." Coincidence might explain it, but it was certainly significant for me, considering that purple is a color I wear often and butterflies are one of my favorite things.

These experiences may be hallucinations or coincidences, but nonetheless, a lot of us are having them. Personally, I'm glad of it.

Margaret Gerner
TCF, St. Louis, MO

CHAPTER XI

QUESTIONS ABOUT GOD'S ROLE MAY SURFACE

your child has died
and only this is certain:
that you will never be
the same again
not what you were
not what you might have been
your child has died
and grief may touch your vision
and new and restless lights
with want and pain
where once your life
found reason strength and peace
your child has died
the face of god is changing:
it may be closer and
more careful now
or may seem cold
and cruel far away
trust in your soul
(how ever bright or somber
how ever calm or fierce)
trust in your soul:
— it will declare
your answer and your hope
in time
in time

Sascha

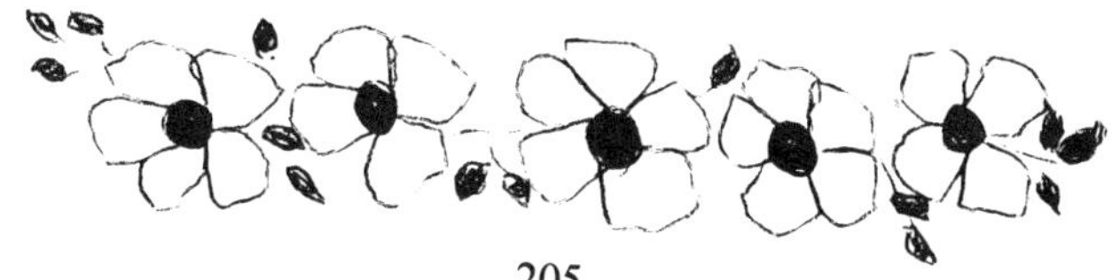

VICTORY OVER GRIEF

I am a vulnerable, mortal being living in an imperfect world. I refuse to believe that a loving God is directing murderers, rapists, greedy warmongers, accidents or illnesses. I cannot be selective and state that those who are fortunate deserve to be or the less fortunate have somehow chosen their fate. I do believe, however, that I as an adult must accept situations beyond my control.

To allow grief to rule my life, expecting unaffected others to mourn with me forever, is to deny the beautiful person my son was. Mark was caring, intelligent, mentally and physically healthy. Each day was to him a marvelous experience and I admired him so much. Upon his death, one of his brothers said that Mark accomplished more in his short lifetime than most do in a full lifetime. I prefer to feel especially blessed that I shared nearly 24 years with him.

I am not yet reconciled to the fact that a fine person dies young while so many miserable ones continue to exist, but I have come to some conclusions that concern bereaved parents.

Why did MY son have to die? Simply because an irresponsible driver chose to speed through a red light.

How many children do I have? Three sons; the eldest, Mark, was killed July 3, 1979.

Mary T. Haynes
TCF, Lexington, KY

PRAYER OF A BEREAVED PARENT

Dear God, I know that man was created in your image, but there are those who so very often appear to think that you were created in ours.

People who mean well have said to those of us who are bereaved parents that you, too, are a bereaved parent and therefore understand our grief. But God, you saw the beginning from the end when your son, Jesus, died, and we cannot. We have only our faith on which to rely, and our faith is so often clouded by our tears.

When you suffered your son, Jesus, to die on the cross, you knew that His death would only serve to bring Him back to you, His Father. But God, our children's deaths have taken them away from us, and the time we must remain in this world without them seems so unbearably long.

And you, Lord Jesus, in your divine love chose to die a mortal death. But our children did not choose to die. You knew the purpose behind your death. But there seems to be no purpose to our children's premature deaths that we, as parents, can determine.

So, while we may boast of being created in your image, we lack the foreknowledge and wisdom to understand why we must grieve. We have only our faith to sustain us, and our faith is so very weak. So, Heavenly Father, please help us to see what we cannot see and to understand what we do not understand so that our grief is not so unbearable. Amen.

David O. Nesnow
TCF, Gastonia, NC

WHAT I WOULD ASK GOD

If I could ask God
One question a day
Where would I start
And what would I say?

After plenty of thought
And limiting to ten
What's the number one
Question with which to begin?

Some people I know
Would see what's in store
But I've learned the lesson
The future to ignore.

Others would ask
About people who've passed
Still others, of nature's things
Both present and past.

All of my questions
Would be of my son
Is he in a place
He can wrestle and run?

When it's cold and he's sick
Who tucks him in tight
And covers him up
On this cold winter's night?

Who hugs and loves his
Boyish young pranks?
Is someone attending
His need for a spank?

Does anyone listen
To those bad elephant jokes?
Does he have someone to play with
To tickle and poke?

Does he know if I could
I'd pass through that door
That I'd gladly die
Just to hold him once more?

Does he see his sister
Her love to know
And his infant brother
Can he watch him grow?

Does he understand for
My daughter and son
As much pain as I feel,
I have to go on?

When the car hit him
Did he see it loom?
Did he know I was there
In that Emergency Room?

My questions are up
I count ten of them
No answers to come
And I did just begin.

If there is a God
Ten questions I'd try
But my number one question
Would have to be - WHY?

Marge Covey
TCF, Madrid, NY

A FATHER'S PRAYER

I am a man, God, and I have been taught that I should be strong and show no weakness. My wife needs me to be strong; I cannot and I must not be weak and lean on her. It is only with you that I can be honest, Lord, and even with you I am ashamed to admit it, but I want to cry. I can feel the tears securely dammed up behind eyes that want to burst.

There is a voice in me that shouts, BE STRONG! BE A MAN! SHOW NO WEAKNESS! SHED NO TEARS! But there is another voice inside that speaks softly and somehow I feel it is your voice, Father. Is it you who tells me that I am also a feeling human being who can cry if I need to? Is it your voice that tells me that maybe my wife needs the tenderness of my tears more than she needs the strength of my muscles?

You are right, Lord, as always. My wife needs to see my grief. She needs to feel the dampness of my tears and know the aching in my heart. Then, just as we became one to create this life, we become one in our grief which mourns this death.

I think I understand, Lord. It is in sharing the awful pain of my grief that I become an even stronger man. It is in sharing my tears that I share my true strength. Oh, God, help me to communicate my deepest and most sensitive feelings to my wife so we may become whole together.

Norman Hagley
TCF, Palestine, TX

TO GOD ABOUT MY SON CLAY

Here is my son, God.
You had one too -
This is what I ask of You.
Take his hand, hold it tight,
Keep him forever in your sight,
Give him comfort, love, and ease.
I pray You will, oh, God, please
Give him joy and peace of mind.
He is gentle, good, and kind.
Let him be happy, his spirit free.
I ask You do all this for me.
I am his mother - I love him so.
That's all, God - the rest you know.

Shirley Blakely Curle
TCF, Alexander, AR

MY PRESENT TO YOU

This is gift giving time, and I want to give you a present - a new concept which has been a comfort to me. I discovered it in a book on language.

The author said that we experience God without knowing it, but our language limits what we attribute to him. In other words, if all we call Him is God, we may see Him only as a remote and omnipotent being. But if we identify God by what He does, we begin to see the role that He plays in our lives and to understand how He reaches out to us.

I asked myself, "How has He related to me as a bereaved parent?" and here are the ways I thought about:

- *as the maker of friendships that have sustained me through my deepest grief*
- *as the Strength that has enabled me to keep on going when I didn't know how I could possibly get through another painful moment*
- *as the Listener who has heard every anguished word I've uttered, as well as my unspoken thoughts*
- *as the Silent Voice that reminded me others were hurting, too, when I thought I was all alone*
- *as the Comforter who caused my friend to call when I needed help and couldn't ask for it*
- *as the Compassionate Friend who knows how I feel.*

This concept can become a living, growing present if you add to the list yourself.

Judy Osgood
TCF, Central Oregon Chapter

PRAYER

God, I can't drag myself to church this morning - please make a house call.

Peter McWilliams
TCF, Dallas, TX

TEACH US TO PRAY

Lord—
I've prayed so much lately,
yet I'm not weary of praying.
I've cried
and begged
and "claimed"
and tried to find
the right "formula"
for healing prayer—
if there is one.

I've pored over Your word
in search of promises
and found so many.
Are they for all of us
all the time?
Does the answer depend
on the pray-er
or the prayed for
or You?

Should we recite Your promises
back to You
to remind You of them?
to convince You that
we know them?
Should we repeat our petitions
for Your benefit
or ours?
Lord, teach us to pray!

After a time, prayer becomes
just sitting in Your presence,
listening
as well as speaking,
waiting
for the touch of peace
and love
and assurance
that our concerns
are safe
in Your hands.

Joan Splettstoesser
TCF, Monte Vista, Co

CHAPTER XII

THINGS WILL BE BETTER

From one who knows

I promise you, my friend,
I promise you
that you will feel
the warmth of spring again
that you will touch
the hands of children
and the lips of lovers
and the tenderness of Christmas again.
But here and now, my friend, I promise you
small consolation:
Some morning you will see
beauty in your sorrow,
comfort in the wealth of love remembered,
courage in the aching tide of days.
I promise you, my friend, I promise you
that you will understand
some day
some day
this pain which taught you
what depth and height
and greatness
and devotion
one life can hold.
YOUR life, my friend.

Sascha

TO SINK OR SWIM

"To sink or swim" are not the only alternatives in life. Many survive just by FLOATING. There were many times after my son died that I did feel as though I was sinking below the waves of grief and I was just too exhausted to try and swim to the other side of that lake of pain. It was at those times that I just simply FLOATED. By floating, it may have taken me longer to reach the shore than it would if I had tried to swim; besides, the shore seemed just so far away that I wouldn't have made it by swimming anyway. But by just floating along with the current, I did not sink and the other side is getting closer all the time.

Verna Smith
TCF, Ft. Worth, TX

POINTS TO PONDER

I don't think I am getting any better." I have heard those words from virtually every bereaved parents I have ever talked to. Bereaved parents don't see their own grief improve because they are with it 24 hours per day. Answer the following questions to see if you are "getting better":
(1) Have I gotten through one hour without crying? (2) Have I gotten through the morning without screaming? (3) Have I slept at least two hours without waking? (4) Have I caught my self smiling instead of crying when I think of my child?

We have to remember to take our grief one step at a time. If you answered "yes" to at least one of the questions above, then you are making progress - you have just taken another step.

Pam Duke
TCF, San Antonio, TX

GETTING BETTER

My tears feel warm on my cheeks now - not burning hot.
Is this a sign I'm "getting better"?
When I cry now I am most often alone -
In the car, or the shower,
Or sometimes taking a walk.
I do not cry in public or feel as much panic.
Is this a sign I'm "getting better"?
I sleep the night through sometimes
And awaken without tears - for awhile.
They come now while I'm brushing my teeth,
Or making coffee
And are always gone before I say "Good Morning."
Is this a sign I'm "getting better"?
Yes, I think so - but when does the pain end?
Perhaps when I no longer ask
Is this a sign I'm "getting better"?

Shirley Blakely Curle
TCF, Central Arkansas, AR

I BRAKE FOR FUN

Maybe I'll have a bumper sticker made and display it on my car.

There's always lots of work for me to do. Sometimes I'm certain I'll never get it all done. I tend to the most pressing things, try to meet deadlines, be prepared for important things. But I BRAKE FOR FUN!

I look for small times of joy and pleasure. After our son was killed, life was so bleak, I knew I HAD to find a little fun somewhere, somehow: an early flower, a pretty cloud, some time with friends who don't upset me, the funnies—anything pleasant to help me smile. It's not a constant search to forget; it's just that I'll stop for happy diversion.

It seems to me that's important, especially during those first few desperate years of surviving your child. GIVE YOURSELF PERMISSION TO BE HAPPY—at least a little. Recognize that it won't be joy unalloyed. Realize that there will be tears, but BRAKE FOR FUN whenever you see something that might be.

Joan D. Schmidt
TCF, Central Jersey Chapter

A LESSON IN GRAMMAR

When your child dies, you soon find yourself back to the basics of English grammar. The question of present, past or future tense takes on added importance and a new dimension. You struggle with the conjugation more so than in elementary school.

The familiar "I am" loses its identity for you find you no longer know who "I am." It is all much more complicated because your present "here and now" suddenly became your past; "is" immediately became "was." Most of the time you find yourself vacillating, not quite sure what the reality of your situation is since the present with its void hurts, the past with its memories hurts, and you can't see much future in your future. There seems no place to hide.

When you have had the time to do the painful but necessary work of creating a life that doesn't include your dead child, you will find once again you have three distinct areas in your life - a present that has less pain in it, a past with memories that now offer comfort, and a future that offers some opportunities for pleasure and happiness. Granted they will differ from what once was, but they're there, nonetheless.

In the meantime, if you're like me, I don't want anybody to quibble with me about whether my son's birthday is or was November 20 because (a) it is and (b) it was and (c) it always will be. And as to whether I have or had two children, (a) I do and (b) I did and (c) I always will have.

You deserve to know the answer to today's pop quiz in English grammar. You may choose (a), (b), (c), or (d) all of the above, and I promise the people who really matter won't mark you wrong, no matter what your choice. So with that out of the way, we can move on to some of the more important courses - like resolving your anger and/or your guilt, for starters. You'll have your Masters in those before we're finished.

Mary Cleckley
TCF, Atlanta, GA

TIME IS A HEALER; IT GIVES YOU THAT PROMISE

Time is what? Painful, too slow, too fast, at a standstill, too short, full of memories, empty, full, healing.

A bereaved parent finds that time is sometimes all they feel that they have left after the death of a child. There is just so much of it and it moves so slowly. There just seems to be too much of it. We go to bed wondering how we will be able to handle the long, seemingly endless darkness. We wait. And wait. And wait.

We wait for the pain to go away. We wait for the time when we will be able to look back in our portfolio of memories and remember the happy times without the pain and anguish that memories sometimes bring. We wait some more.

People tell us (over and over and over) that time will take care of things. We are told that time will make us forget. Forget? Who wants to forget? We want to be able to handle it and want to be able to live again. But forget? You've got to be kidding. I lost a baby that I never saw. According to "the world who has never been there" the loss of our infant daughter should have been easy to forget. It (according to "them") should have been the best thing for me to do. I mean, forgetting something is supposed to be the best way to get over it, isn't it?

Well, in my case, I did not want to forget. I did not want to get over it! I carried that precious baby girl for months. I felt her kick. She was mine and I did not want to forget her! But, like I said, time was supposed to take care of things. I didn't believe it. I didn't think I would ever stop hurting. But I did!

Time is a healer. It is not miraculous. It takes care of the pain and the hurting, but it doesn't take away the memories. But it does help you put things in perspective and gives you the opportunity to reflect without the pain and anguish. How much time does it take? I wish I could tell you so that you could mark it on your calendar and know that on a certain day or month or year you would wake up feeling great. But it doesn't work that way.

Each time a newly bereaved parent asks me, "How long before..." I always tell them that each person is different. But however much time it does take, be sure to be patient with yourself, your spouse, and your surviving children. Simply speaking, it takes as much time as it takes. But don't rush it. And for goodness sake don't let anyone else rush you either.

Time is a healer. I give you that promise. But time is sometimes very slow, especially when you are taking the time to recover from the loss of a child. But it does pass. Each day, each night that passes you are a little closer to the time when you will find joy in life again. Be patient with yourself. You will make it!

Deby Amos
TCF, Anniston, AL

IN CELEBRATION OF LAUGHTER

Today I laughed,
a throaty little giggle,
a tiny laugh
this first time
since you died.

Today I laughed,
no hearty chuckle,
a light laugh
this first time
since you died.

Today I laughed,
a little laugh,
little laugh
since you left.

Today I laughed,
a tinkling laugh,
echoing from my soul.
I was happy
it is a beginning . . .

Toby Sue Shaw
TCF, Stamford, CT

CHAPTER XIII

THE NON-BEREAVED CAN HELP TOO

I want to cry.
Just sometime, let me cry.
Do not demand
that constant smile from me.

I know you are
uneasy with my tears.
I need to cry.
Please, do not go away.

I promise you
that I will smile again.
Tomorrow I
will be as light as air.

But hold me now
and let my sorrow be.
Just for today,
this moment: let me cry.

Sascha

PLEASE, SEE ME THROUGH MY TEARS

You asked, "How are you doing?"

As I told you, tears came to my eyes. You immediately began to talk again, your eyes looked away from me, your speech picked up, and all the attention you had given me went away.

How am I doing? I do better when people will listen to my response, even though I may shed a tear or two, for I so want their attention; but to be ignored because I have in me pain which is indescribable to anyone who has not been there makes me hurt and feel angry. So when you look away, I am again alone with it.

Really, tears are not a bad sign, you know! They're nature's way of helping me to heal. They relieve some of the stress of sadness. I know you fear that asking how I'm doing brought this sadness to me. No, you're wrong, the memory of my son's death will always be with me, only a thought away.

It's just that my tears make my pain more visible to you, but you did not give me the pain; it's just there. When I cry, could it be that you feel helpless? You're not, you know. When I feel your permission to allow my tears to flow, you've helped me more than you can know. You need not verbalize your support of my tears; your silence as I cry is my key, do not fear.

Your listening with your heart to "How are you doing?" helps relieve the pain, because once I allow the tears to come and go, I feel lighter. Talking to you releases things I've been wanting to say aloud, and then there's space for a touch of joy in my life

Honest, when I tear up and cry, that doesn't mean I'll cry forever - maybe just a minute or two. Then I'll wipe the tears away, and sometimes you'll even find I'm laughing at something funny ten minutes later. When I hold back my tears, my throat grows tight, my chest aches, and my stomach begins to knot up because I'm trying to protect you from my tears. Then we both hurt; me, because I've kept the pain inside and it's a shield against our closeness, and then you hurt because suddenly we're distant. Please take my hand, and I promise not to cry forever (it's physically impossible, you know).

When you see me through my tears, then we can be close again.

Kelly Osmont
TCF, Portland, OR

You once did something for me
More meaningful than the greatest of deeds:
You held me in your arms and let me cry.

Bonnie Jison
TCF, Topeka, KS

WHEN YOU WISH UPON A STAR

Every time that I am in a group of bereaved parents, I hear people say things like "I wish my child hadn't died" or "I wish I had him back." Those wishes, unfortunately, can never come true.

The other wish I hear is "I wish my friends (or church, or neighbors, or relatives) understood what I am going through and were more supportive. This is a wish that has some possibility of coming true if we are able to be honest and assertive with the people around us. What do we wish others understood about the loss of our child? Here is a partial list of such wishes:

1. I wish you would not be afraid to speak my child's name. My child lived and was important and I need to hear his name.

2. If I cry or get emotional if we talk about my child, I wish you knew that it isn't because you have hurt me; the fact that my child died has caused my tears. You have allowed me to cry and I thank you. Crying and emotional outbursts are healing.

3. I wish you wouldn't "kill" my child again by removing from your home his pictures, artwork, or other remembrances.

4. I will have emotional highs and lows, ups and downs. I wish you wouldn't think that if I have a good day my grief is all over or that if I have a bad day, I need psychiatric counseling.

5. I wish you knew that the death of a child is different from other losses and must be viewed separately. It is the ultimate tragedy and I wish you wouldn't compare it to your loss of a parent, a spouse, or a pet.

6. Being a bereaved parent is not contagious, so I wish you wouldn't shy away from me.

7. I wish you knew that all of the "crazy" grief reactions I am having are in fact very normal. Depression, anger, frustration, hopelessness, and the questioning of values and beliefs are to be expected following the death of a child.

8. I wish you wouldn't expect my grief to be over in six months. The first few years are going to be exceedingly traumatic for us. As with alcoholics, I will never be "cured" or a "former bereaved parent," but will forevermore be a "recovering bereaved parent."

9. I wish you understood the physical reactions to grief. I may gain weight or lose weight, sleep all the time or not at all, develop a host of illnesses and be accident prone, all of which may be related to my grief.

10. Our child's birthday, the anniversary of his death, and holidays are terrible times for us. I wish you could tell us that you are thinking about our child on these days, and if we get quiet and withdrawn, just know we are thinking about our child and don't try to coerce us into being cheerful.

11. It is normal and good that most of us reexamine our faith, values, and beliefs after losing a child. We will question things we have been taught all our lives and hopefully come to some new understanding with our God. I wish you would let me tangle with my religion without making me feel guilty.

12. I wish you wouldn't offer me drinks or drugs. These are just temporary crutches and the only way I can get through this grief is to experience it. I have to hurt before I can heal.

13. I wish you understood that grief changes people. I am not the same person I was the moment before my child died and I never will be that person again. If you keep waiting for me to "get back to my old self," you will stay frustrated. I am a new creature with new thoughts, dreams, aspirations, values and beliefs. Please try to get to know the new me - maybe you'll like me still.

Instead of sitting around and waiting for our wishes to come true, we have an obligation to teach people some of the things we have learned about our grief. We can teach these lessons with great kindness, believing that people have good intentions and want to do what is right, but just don't know what to do with us.

Do you remember the result when Pavlov, the famous psychologist, rewarded his dogs for doing the right thing? Their behavior repeated! If a neighbor sends a plate of cookies on the day of your child's birth, tell her how much you appreciate her remembering your child. If a relative jots a note in a Christmas card and says he is thinking about you during this difficult time, write back and thank him for acknowledging your pain. If by accident a friend mentions your child's name and it makes you cry, you may not be able to thank them at that time, but you can tell them later how important it is to talk about your child. Whether one of your wishes is fulfilled by accident or through great sensitivity, reward others for what they have done for you. Chances are good that they will repeat these kindnesses on other occasions, and perhaps your wish of having more understanding friends and relatives will come true.

Elaine Grier
TCF, Atlanta, GA

DON'T THEY KNOW?

"It's a good way to die."
Don't they know there is no good way for a child to die? Can't they understand that there's nothing good about his being snatched away from our life?

"Remember, every thing is God's will."
Don't they know I can't understand how God could cause me so much despair? Don't they understand that I can't accept this as God's will?

"All things work together for the good of those who love God."
Don't they know I'm not sure I can love God who robbed me of my child? Can't they understand I'm very angry at God, who treated me so unfairly?

"Your child is better off. He's gone to heaven, where he'll have eternal peace."
Don't they know I can't be relieved to know he's in heaven when I ache so to have him back? Can't they understand that I feel his death is an injustice, not a godsend?

"Count your blessings."
Don't they know that in this state of mind I can't in my wildest dreams consider all this pain, this anger, this emptiness, this frustration, a blessing?

"If you look around you, you'll find someone worse off than you are."
Don't they know right now I can't imagine anyone worse off than I am?

"You're so lucky. You had several wonderful years together."
Don't they know we should have had many, many more years together? His life was only beginning.

"Think of all your previous memories."
Don't they know how much it hurts to live with nothing more than memories? Can't they understand that because our love was so great, the pain is more intense.

"Keep your chin up."
Don't they know how hard it is to do that when I really want to cry, to wail, to scream at the injustice that has been dealt me?

"You can have other children."
Don't they know we may very well have another baby (or maybe we can't), but it will be another child, not a replacement for our child who died? Each child is unique and irreplaceable. Having another child will not erase the pain we feel at losing this special child.

"You must put it behind you and get on with your life."
Don't they know we don't hurt by choice when our children die? I haven't met a bereaved parent yet who wasn't really weary of the hurting.

"If there's anything I can do, let me know."
Don't they know they shouldn't wait for me to "let them know." Can't they understand that my mind is so numb I can't even think of what needs to be done?

"You're young. You'll be able to make a new life for yourself."
Don't they know a new life is the very last thing I want, that all I want right now is the life we had?

"Time will heal."
Don't they know how time is dragging for me now, that every minute seems like an hour and every hour like a day? Can't they understand how frightening it is to face the rest of my life without my child?

Don't they know? Of course these wonderful, concerned, well-meaning friends don't know. They can only guess how I feel. They haven't personally known (thank God) the disbelief, the shock, the anger, the depression that has filled my heart and soul since my child died. They don't know that the words I need to hear are:
"I know you must be hurting terribly. You had such a good life together, the pain must be awful. Don't be embarrassed to cry. I know you need to express your despair, your anger, your frustration. I know it must be hard for you to believe that God is a loving God who will support you through this horrible tragedy."
They can't know words aren't necessary, that just being there, holding my hand, crying with me, or listening to me would be much more comforting than the words they feel they must say.
Can't they understand? Of course, they can't understand.

Anita Gordon
TCF, Colorado Springs, CO

I KNOW YOU ARE LISTENING TO ME WHEN:

You come quietly into my private world
and let me be.

You really try to understand me even
when I am not making sense.

You grasp my point even when it is
against your sincere convictions.

You realize that the hour I took from you
has left you a bit tired and drained.

You allow me the dignity of making my
own decisions even though you think
they might be wrong.

You do not take my problem from me
but allow me to deal with it in my
own way.

You hold back from giving me a word
of "good advice."

You do not offer me religious solace
when you sense I am not ready for it.

You give me enough room to discover
for myself what is really going on.

You accept my gift of gratitude by
telling me how it makes you feel
good being helpful.

Glen Crawford
TCF, Perth, Australia

BEING THERE

Do you know of someone
whose precious child has died?
Perhaps she is a neighbor or friend
with whom you can confide.
You assume that she is suffering
a tragedy so deep,
That there is nothing you can do
since all she does is weep.
You feel that if you see her
there is nothing you can say
That would make her precious child come back
or make the pain go away.
And if by chance you meet her
and have to face her grief,
You'll do your very best
to make this meeting brief.
You'll talk about the weather
or the lady down the lane,
But, you'll never mention her child -
that would cause her too much pain!
And when the funeral's over,
and all is said and done,
You'll go home to your family,
and she'll be all alone.
She'll go on, she'll be all right, time heals -
or so it seems,
While she's left alone to pick up the pieces
of her shattered life and dreams.

OR . . .

You can open up your heart
and find that special place
Where compassion and true giving
are awaiting your embrace.
"Today I'm thinking of you
in a very special way,"
Or, how about "I Love You!"
are some loving things to say.
Sometimes a very simple task
like picking up the phone,
Can help her feel not-so-quite
desperately alone.
Whatever comes from a genuine heart
cannot be said in vain,
For the truth is, it's these very things
that lessen her great pain.
And when you let her talk about
her child who is now dead,
You'll know this is far greater
than anything you've said.
So, will you reach out with all your soul
and let her know you care?
For in the end, there's no substitute
for simply BEING THERE!

Debi Pettigrew
TCF, Tampa, FL

CHAPTER XIV

WE NEED NOT WALK ALONE

This is a day when I can't laugh or cry.
This is a day when I keep asking "why?"
This is a day when I regret and grieve.
This is a day when I will not believe
That love and joy and hope were ever true.

And then, my friend,
I do remember you.
And then, my friend,
My life returns from stone.
And then, my friend,
I touch my heart and know
This is a day we need not walk alone.

Sascha

HOPES AND WISHES

When you attend a National Compassionate Friends Conference for the first time, you bring many hopes and wishes for what the conference might offer you. We hope your expectations are met and even surpassed. And as you leave, we have some special hopes and wishes for you.

- to the newly bereaved, we wish you patience - patience with yourselves in the painful weeks, months, even years ahead.

- to the bereaved siblings who have joined us, we wish you and your parents a new understanding of each other's needs and the beginning of good communication.

- to those of you who are single parents, we wish you the inner resources we know you will need to cope, often alone, with your loss.

- to those of you who are plagued with guilt, we wish you the reassurance that you did the very best you could under the circumstances and that your child knew that.

- to those of you who have suffered multiple losses - those who have experienced the death of more than one child - we wish you the endurance you will need to fight your way back to a meaningful life once again.

- To those of you who are deeply depressed, we wish you the first steps out of the "valley of the shadow."

- to those experiencing marital difficulties after the death of your child, we wish you a special willingness and ability to communicate with each other.

- to all chapter leaders, especially those experiencing various degrees of burnout, we wish you renewal in both body and spirit.

- to all regional coordinators, we wish you 37-hour days. You need them!

- to all the fathers, we wish you the ability to express your grief, to move beyond society's conditioning, to cry.

- to those with few or no memories of your child, perhaps because you suffered through a stillbirth, a miscarriage, or infant death, we wish you the sure knowledge that your child is a ***person*** *and that your grief is real.*

- to those of you who have experienced the death of an only child or of all your children, we offer you our eternal gratitude for serving as such an inspiration to the rest of us.

- to those of you who are unable to cry, we wish you healing tears.

- to those of you who are tired, exhausted from grieving, we wish you the strength to face just one more hour, just one more day.

- to those who return to homes and communities where you find no support or understanding, we ask you to take with you the very special love that fills this room, and to draw on it when you need it most in the days ahead.

- and to all others with special needs that we have not mentioned, we wish you the understanding you need and the assurance that you are loved.

- and, finally, to all of you, we wish safe travel to your homes and many warm memories of our special time this weekend as members of the TCF Family and the reminder that "We need not walk alone. We are The Compassionate Friends."

Joe Rosseau, President
The Compassionate Friends
Said at the 1985 Buffalo National
Conference, Buffalo, NY

YOU ARE NOT ALONE

We know the heartache
that you bear
We've felt the pain
cause we've been there
We share a bond
of infinite sorrow
A hope for peace—
strength for tomorrow.

A time will come
when you'll seek relief
Solace and comfort
to ease your grief
We welcome you —
we shall be there
We understand —
We've much to share.

TCF, Scranton, PA

TOGETHER WE'LL WALK THE STEPPING STONES

Come, take my hand, the road is long.
We must travel by stepping stones.
No, you're not alone, I'll go with you.
I know the road well, I've been there.
Don't fear the darkness, I'll be there with you.
We must take one step at a time
But remember we may have to stop awhile.
It is a long way to the other side
And there may be obstacles.

We have many stones to cross, some are bigger than others,
Shock, denial and anger to start.
Then comes guilt, despair and loneliness.
It's a hard road to travel, but it must be done.
It's the only way to reach the other side.

Come, slip your hand in mine.
What? Oh, yes, it's strong, I've held so many hands like yours.
Yes, mine was one time small and weak like yours.
Once, you see, I had to take someone's hand in order to take the first step.
Oops! You've stumbled; go ahead and cry.
Don't be ashamed; I understand.
Let's wait here awhile and get your breath.
When you're stronger we'll go on, one step at a time.
There's no need to hurry.
Say, it's nice to hear you laugh. Yes, I agree,
The memories you shared are good.
Look, we're halfway there now; I can see the other side.
It looks so warm and sunny.
Oh, have you noticed, we're nearing the last stone and you're standing alone?
We've reached the other side.

But wait, look back, someone is standing there.
They are alone and want to cross the stepping stones.
I'd better go, they need my help.
What? Are you sure?
Why, yes, go ahead, I'll wait, you know the way, you've been there.
Yes, I agree, it's your turn, my friend—
To help someone else cross the stepping stones.

Barb Williams
TCF, Ft. Wayne, IN

CONTRIBUTORS

In Memory of Adam Scott Cole
Carol Gray Cole and Karyn

In Memory of Sheila Coleman
Jerry and Sylvia Coleman

In Memory of Michael James DeMarco
Jack and Desiree DeMarco

In Memory of Malinda Louise Donahey
Dorothy L. Donahey

In Memory of Patrick Hennessey Flanagan
Susan and Sean Flanagan

In Memory of Paula Marie Goodrich
John and Therese Goodrich and Family

In Memory of Jimmy, Nathan and Ethan Heavilin
Marilyn and Glen Heavilin

In Memory of Amy Gwynn Hess
Janice and Harry W. Hess

In Memory of Jessica Lynn Hess
Janice and Harry W. Hess

In Memory of Alison Kaplan
Bill and Judy Kaplan and Family

In Memory of Andrea Levine
Phyllis Levine

In Memory of Michael Joseph Michalek
Dennis and Elaine Michalek and Family

In Memory of Donna Lee Moore
Don, Carole, Amy and Alex Moore

In Memory of Mark William Pfeiffer
Gene, Beverly and Kristina Pfeiffer

In Memory of Tracy Ralph Saulisberry
Chuck and Jo Saulisberry

In Memory of Robert George Slowiak
Ray and Yvonne Slowiak and Family

CONTRIBUTORS

In Memory of Stephen Mark Vervaet
Nancy, Tom, Sandy and Phil Vervaet

In Memory of Walter O. Washington
Jane B. Washington

INDEX

PAGE NO.

The Compassionate Friends Publications

The Grief of Parents . . . When a Child Dies: For those who have experienced the death of a child, often the first question asked is how is it possible to survive such a devastating experience. Learning about the grieving process does not take the pain of grief away, but it can help lift the burden of isolation, fear, and confusion about what bereaved parents are experiencing. This booklet covers many of these important issues. It is short enough to read when concentration is difficult but long enough to offer significant insight into the grieving process. ($1.75)

When a Baby Dies: Written by parents who each experienced the death of a baby, this booklet addresses some of the immediate decisions that need to be made following the death of an infant. It is appropriate to give to a parent who is still in the hospital. This book offers what the authors refer to as a collection of "signposts and landmarks" for parents struggling to come to grips with their loss. ($2.25)

Now Childless: A collection of sensitive and insightful articles and poetry that specifically addresses the needs and concerns of parents who have experienced the death of an only child or all of their children. The authors, both whom experienced the death of an only child, recognize both the unique issues parents must cope with and the communalities of their grief experience. This is an important book for bereaved parents as well as those who love them and care about their healing. ($6.95)

- To order these books, please write or call the National Office for a complimentary *Resource Guide* which lists these publications as well as many other bereavement resources.

The Compassionate Friends Newsletters

The National Newsletter: Published quarterly, the 8-page *National Newsletter* features poetry and original articles by bereaved parents. Also included are book reviews, timely information about the national TCF program and newly published grief-related resources.

The Sibling Newsletter: Published quarterly, the *Sibling Newsletter* is a mix of informative articles, stories of personal experiences and poetry written by and for bereaved siblings.

- To subscribe to either newsletter please write or call the National Office for a complimentary copy.

The Compassionate Friends Brochures

The Compassionate Friends publishes 18 brochures covering a wide range of grief-related issues. Each pamphlet is discussed, debated, and thoughtfully written by bereaved parents. These pamphlets offer valuable information about the grief experience and deal with the problems and concerns of bereaved parents in a frank and forthright manner.

When a Child Dies (TCF General Brochure)
Understanding Grief: When a Child Dies
Dolor Y Comprension
Stillbirth, Miscarriage and Infant Death: Understanding Grief
Suggestions for Medical Personnel: When a Child Dies
Surviving Your Child's Suicide
Suggestions for Clergy
Suggestions for Teachers and School Counselors
When an Employee Is Grieving
Principles of TCF
When a Brother or Sister Dies
How Can I Help?
When a Co-Worker Is Grieving
For First Responders: The Sudden Death of a Child
Cuando Muere Un Nino
When a Grandchild Dies . . . Understanding Grief
Suggestions for Funeral Directors
The Grief of Stepparents . . . When a Child Dies

- To receive a complimentary copy of any of these pamphlets, please write or call the National Office.

The Resource Guide: This 8-page free catalog is available to bereaved parents and those who provide support and assistance to them. All of the material presented has been reviewed and found to be helpful in understanding and assisting parents through the healing necessary following the death of their child.

The Compassionate Friends
National Office
P.O. Box 3696
Oak Brook, IL 60522-3696
708/990-0010